San Diego

An Illustrated History

SAN DIEGO

An Illustrated History

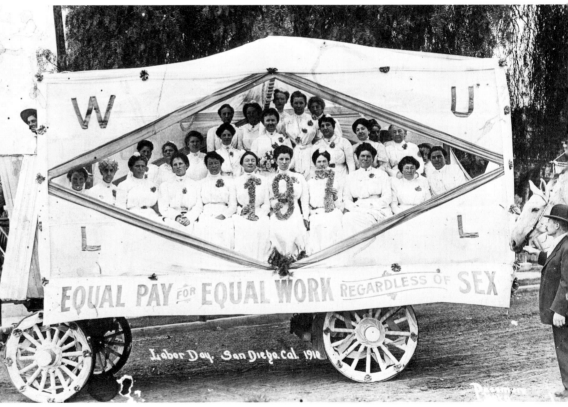

by Ray Brandes

A Rosebud Book
Los Angeles

First published in 1981 by Rosebud Books, a division of the Knapp Press, 5455 Wilshire Boulevard, Los Angeles, California.

Design by Jill Casty

Library of Congress Cataloging in Publication Data

Brandes, Ray, 1924-
    San Diego, an illustrated history.

    Bibliography: p.
    1. San Diego (Calif.)—History—Pictorial works.
    2. San Diego (Calif.)—Description—Views. I. Title.
F869.S22B73   979.4'98   81-6496
ISBN 0-86558-006-5   AACR2

To Ted and Mary Brandes, my parents,
To Fred and Tean Brandes and Ed and Nettie Deeter,
 who whetted my interest in archaeology
   and history
To the more than fifty graduate students who were gracious enough
to allow me to direct their master's theses in history at the
   University of San Diego
    and especially to
my wife, Irma Montijo, and my children, Elena María, Elisa Ann,
  Laura Raquel, Raymond Anthony, Claudia Renee,
   Marta Denise and Paula Nicole

Acknowledgments

IN A WORK OF this nature the contributions of others are paramount. Some very outstanding works have already been published on the history of our city. Additionally several university professors and local authors have made the results of their research available, some of which should find its way into print. Numbers of college students write special papers or take part in programs which contribute information. This illustrated history is, therefore, only one contribution to a better understanding of our past.

This book was conceived after Donald Ackland, publisher at Rosebud Books, worked with Carleton Winslow, AIA , Professor, California State University at San Luis Obispo on his beautiful work *The Enchanted Hill.* Carleton had worked with me at the University of San Diego writing his master's thesis on his father's work as an architect on the Panama-California Exposition in San Diego.

The staff of Rosebud Books brought together the bits and pieces to make the puzzle come together. I owe much to Helen Abbott, editor, for smoothing out many manuscript and photograph arrangements. Leilani Austria took marvelous photographs of the current scene and did copy work for the color section (and got a taste of field archaeology in the process). Laura LiPuma designed the dust jacket and Jill Casty designed the book itself.

The writing of the textual material and the photo essays comes as much from the rich files of *The San Diego Union* and other newspapers and the works in the bibliography as it does from

my own experiences of nearly six decades in *This Fantastic City*, to steal a title from Shelley Higgins. I have tried not to editorialize or opine, but a bit of that comes from each of us who is tied inextricably to San Diego.

In the selection of illustrative material there are many individuals who went out of their way to retrieve what appears as the heart of this work. Larry and Jane Booth, recognized authorities in the field of photographic preservation, Sidney Lynch and Dr. Richard Esparza of the San Diego Historical Society (Title Insurance & Trust Collection) were of much help. I thank Mary Ward, Historian, County Parks and Recreation Department, Virginia Mannasse, Mr. and Mrs. Joseph Jessop and Frank Wolden of Centre City Development Corporation for providing photographs. Rhoda Kruse and the staff of the California Room, San Diego Public Library, Main Branch, gave many clues and much aid to the pulling together of material for use, both literary and photographic.

I am indebted to my peers and colleagues who read parts of the manuscript and made valuable suggestions. Dr. James R. Moriarty III, Elizabeth McPhail, and Michael Stepner added advice here and there.

As a professor of history and an archaeologist who has taught more than twenty years, I have received ideas and thoughts about San Diego from literally hundreds of students. Whether we walked

the streets photographing and describing buildings for a cultural resource survey, whether we were engaged in archaeology in New or Old Town, whether we sat in a round table looking at San Diego from various perspectives, ideas always flowed forth from the students, the future leaders of our community. I thank them for enriching my own background for this work. And, to my good friend Susan Sullivan, Director of Graduate Career Programs at the University of San Diego, there are many long overdue thanks for help over the past six years: she has arranged historical programs, served as a research assistant, and is a historian in her own right.

Thanks are due to the following individuals for assisting me in locating photographs or adding information which would help me with the text or photographic essays: Frank A. Wolden of Centre City Development Corporation, Torrey Enterprises, Inc., Greg Chandler of the Maritime Museum of San Diego, Janet Fireman of the Los Angeles County Museum of Natural History, John Henderson, AIA, Susan Erzinger, Julia Erwin, James E. Moriarty IV, Denise Newlon, and Judith Weiss.

CONTENTS

Introduction

SAN DIEGO, CALIFORNIA is a spectacular city on the rim of the Pacific Ocean occupying 290 square miles in a county that spreads out over 4,258 square miles of land. For 70 miles along the coast from San Clemente to the Mexican Border is accessible shoreline; 80 miles inland is the Imperial County line. In the back country, the mountains crest at 6,500 feet. The break between the slope to the ocean and the desert country on the other side is picturesque from the Palomar, Cuyamaca, and Laguna ranges.

The mesa land seems inexhaustible, and growth follows these smooth and flat areas. The valleys which run down to the bay and the ocean could be squandered one by one if growth becomes the cause for use. But preservationists help create new parks and recreational areas out of the reservoir of space. San Diego is a collection of communities. Each should preserve its own unique qualities for future generations.

In recent times the ethnic character of the city has changed greatly, as it has in the rest of California. The Hispanic people are no less than one third of the population. Their heritage is found in street names, language, food, dress, and music. Predictions are that by the turn of the century the minority in California will comprise the majority, in part because of the influx of people from Mexico.

Vietnamese, Indo-Chinese, Laotians, Russians, Poles, Hungarians, Bulgarians, and Czechoslovakians are mixing some-

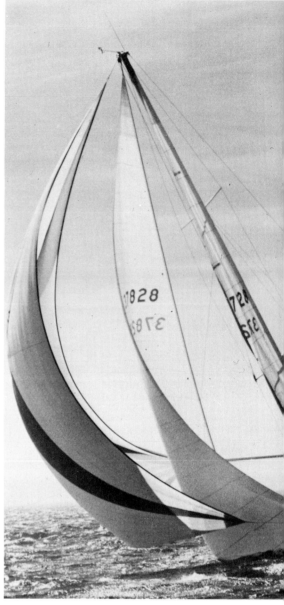

Previous Page: Entrants riding a Cleveland motorbike and unicycle participated in an imaginative 1924 parade. Above: Palm trees surrounded a festive Christmas tree in Horton Plaza, where soldiers and sailors gathered for this 1917 photograph.

San Diego
An Illustrated History

14

times easily, sometimes not so comfortably with the larger community. But this ethnic infusion is the very lifeblood of a vigorous nation and a city enriched over and over again by the process. The beauty is the interplay among the people, the willingness to help one another, the acceptance of individuals whose culture is different.

San Diego: An Illustrated History is meant to explain how San Diego became the city which might well serve as the model for future cities. Born with certain good fortune, it has a mild climate, a good harbor with easy access to distant ports, and clean air and clear skies. Now low-rise buildings preserve the view; there is a mixture of peoples of every kind; and the economy is based upon tourism, government systems, and highly selective industries with a concern about the environment. A succession of men and women blessed with the minds and motivation to do something for their region have brought San Diego to the point where it can be called "America's Finest City."

Above Left: Rigorous sailing competitions take place nearly every weekend in San Diego and Mission bays. Both large and small craft are available for rent from the numerous hotels and marinas. Above: Restored buildings of the

Gaslamp Quarter National Historic District cover seventeen downtown city blocks, instilling both conservationists and residents with renewed pride. The refurbished quarters provide alternative office space in the city which is increasingly becoming high rise. Above Right: The curving Coronado Bay Bridge connects San Diego with the once desolate

Coronado peninsula, where a nineteenth-century developer materialized his dream for a million-dollar hotel and residential community.

Like their present-day successors, ancient La Jollans preferred living on the rocky ridges which stabbed the coastline, commanding a lucid view of their domain and providing access to the life-giving sea. These cliffs represented the first view of the mythical "Calafia" to sixteenth-century Spanish sailors seeking riches and wealth in the New World.

CHAPTER I

The Age of Discovery

AT SOME DISTANT time in the past, man and woman crossed a land bridge in the Bering Strait, making their way from Asia in search of game in North America. Down the Mackenzie Mountain Range and the eastern slope of the Rocky Mountains they tracked the mammoth into an unfamiliar frontier.

No mass migrations took place. Small groups of wanderers trailed their quarry. Some hunters moved to the eastern limits of land while others pushed southward where their descendants created civilizations.

Present-day desert regions once held resources and wildlife; there some prehistoric men stayed. Other peoples moved over the Sierra Nevadas and followed the coastal ranges down the Pacific slope, searching for places to live.

From about 9,000 B.C. to 6,000 B.C., these first Americans, now called the San Dieguito, came into Southern California and adapted to the environment. In places along lake shores, near streams or water holes they settled. Others chose mesas and ridges for campsites while some preferred to remain in the lower mountains. Until about 6,000 B.C., their pattern of existence centered on hunting and fishing. They gathered semiaquatic plants from the edges of basins and lake beds. Game, fish, and fowl added protein to their diets.

Between 6,000 B.C. and the time of Christ, more people worked their way into the southlands to mix with the Indians already present. These "La Jollans" left signs of their occupation.

Historians speculate as to whether Sir Francis Drake ever entered San Diego Harbor. Several years after his circumnavigational voyage aboard the Golden Hinde, *Drake seized the treasure-laden* Santa Ana *off San Lucas in Baja California with his vessels* Content *and* Desire, *possibly taking refuge in the port of San Diego. This engraving by Thomas de Leu cites Drake's age at forty-three.*

San Diego
An Illustrated History

18

Like man of the twentieth century, they sought out the best places to live — on ridges with a view of their domain and along the surfline where they could gather seafood or raft out into deep water to fish. During certain seasons they migrated into the back country to gather pine nuts, berries, and seeds, all of which could be ground up to serve as bulk food.

Hunters and gatherers were mobile and did not practice agriculture. In time as they watched native plants grow, cared for them, and learned to harvest them at the right times, they became more permanently attached to one place and there they stayed.

Early men have been traced through their artifacts, including chipped stone and rock circles, but remains found are few and their meaning elusive. Like other organic remains, hide clothing, wooden arrow shafts, and even man's brittle bones returned to the earth.

Diegueño or Kumeyaay Indians drifted into this region about 1,000 B.C., bringing different ideas and customs. They mixed with the Indians already here. Their descendants were the people who met the Europeans who first came to San Diego in 1542.

In spite of an amazing amount of archaeological work in the San Diego area, hard data about ancient man in this region have provided few new interpretations of the region's history. The information is better found in the written record of the Europeans than in the fragile nature of man's remains in the soil. Maps show names of bands, locations, and numbers of Indian *rancherías*.

The coastal tribes remained virtually out of contact with other Indians of the Southwest who had long since built multistoried apartment-like cities with ball courts and with canal systems to irrigate the arid regions. The Laguna Mountain Range just east of the Pacific Ocean, coupled with major deserts, cut off contact among peoples, which resulted in the exchange of few ideas and traditions. The customs and traits brought by the Hispanics would, therefore, be indelibly imprinted on the Indians already living in the land.

Other evidence that the Indian way of life remained fairly rudimentary is found in the *diarios* of Spaniards. In 1542, Juan Rodríguez Cabrillo's men gave little attention to describing the Indians, reporting only that they engaged in a brief skirmish near the beach and that the Indians refused to wear clothing offered them. The significance of the meetings lay in gestures made by the natives who signaled with bows and arrows that men rode horses in the back country and killed the Indians — they had already heard of other Spaniards traveling to the east.

Discovery and exploration of unknown lands has always been a part of man's dreams. Centuries before the discovery of the New World by the Spaniards, men left home to sail out into the unknown. The pioneering adventurers often returned to tell stories of mysterious and strange regions, and many of these tales grew into myths.

In their search for new lands the Spanish explorers taught the rest of the world a lesson in navigation and seamanship as they struck out for all corners of the world. While other nations soon became as enthusiastic as Spain about the possibilities of finding riches in unknown places, Spain became the leader as her vessels probed the New World and landed men and weapons wherever they could touch the shores.

Rapidly Spanish civilization was planted in Mexico and South America. The crown ordered soldiers to move overland from the Valley of Mexico in a three pronged march northward. One wing of the military drove along the Pacific shore of the Mexican mainland. Here Spaniards built bases for shipbuilding. From ports such as Guadalajara, Mazatlan, and San Blas, the Spaniards extended their quest for wealth.

Early conquistadors Hernándo Santotís, Sebastián Vizcaíno, and Isidro Atondo y Antillon looked for and found pearls in the Gulf of California (the Sea of Cortéz).

Hernándo Cortéz looked for the mythical "Strait of Anían" to the East Indies, and he, too, fished for pearls in the Gulf of California. One of his lieutenants, Bernal Diaz del Castillo, referred to the place "California" in his writings.

In 1539, Francisco de Ulloa may have given the name "California" to this land, but three years later Juan Rodríguez Cabrillo

The sixteenth century belonged to those seafaring soldiers of fortune as the twentieth century belongs to the astronauts probing and charting unknown lands. Their vessels included the classic Spanish galleon (above left) which carried thirty-six guns and the smaller caravels (above) typical of those which carried Columbus, Da Gama and Cabot. Many of the vessels of this period were clumsy, rolled terribly, and pitched, but they managed to withstand rough weather.

Age of Discovery

19

Left: The Cahuilla Indians wove a rattlesnake design into this basket, part of a collection at the Southwest Museum.

Above Left: A typical temporary summer dwelling of the Diegueño and Luiseno Indians in the nineteenth and early twentieth centuries was constructed of fragile willow or tule which grew in swamps or near the shoreline. Winter homes were always built of adobe. Above Right: Edward Harvey Davis posed with Chief Yellow Sky in this 1912 photograph. Davis's studies of the back country resulted in a number of publications useful to anthropologists today. Above Middle: Chipped stonework and arrowheads were recovered from various southern California sites.

San Diego
An Illustrated History

20

first sighted San Diego harbor from the sea. A Portuguese navigator in the hire of Spain, he commanded two vessels, the *San Salvador* and the *Victoria*, which entered the bay on September 28, 1542. On the eve of the feast day of St. Michael the Archangel, he named the place San Miguel.

Year after year vessels in the Manila Galleon trade had followed the Japanese currents from the Orient to make landfall off Cape Mendocino and sail down the coast to Acapulco. Yet a curious lull remains in the historical record. Until perhaps Sir Francis Drake himself sailed the coastline, records telling of voyages remained hidden in the Archives of the Indies and in the Archivo General de la Nación.

Sebastián Vizcaíno had sailed from Acapulco as *comandante* of the *San Diego, Santo Tomás,* and the *Tres Reyes,* to rename San Diego on November 12, 1602, for the patron saint of the flagship on that feast day of San Diego de Alcalá.* Wherever Catholic explorers stepped ashore, as did these men from another continent, their priests "pitched a suitable tent to serve as a church," and celebrated a solemn Mass.

A gifted priest, Father Antonio de la Ascensión, one of the three priests of the Discalced order of Carmelites who had sailed with Vizcaíno, wrote of the good water and fish of all kinds caught with seine and hooks. He saw at San Diego rabbits, hares, deer, very large quail, royal ducks, thrushes, and many other kinds of birds. In exchange for biscuits and fish, the Indians gave the Spaniards skin of martens, wild cats, and other animals. They devoured an abundance of white fish, sea fish, oysters, clams, lobsters, crabs, and sardines harvested from the ocean.

*Spanish for St. James of Alcalá; St. Didacus of the Roman Catholic Church.

Vizcaíno's voyage marked the end of an era in which the search for the mythical had been paramount in the minds of the explorers, but colonization would not take place for 167 more years.

Spain was not prepared to settle California. Her emphasis was on a larger, growing Spanish empire which included outposts in the Pacific and the Orient. Her men of armor and robes had exploration and Christianity on their minds, but they were not equipped to move into the next stage of securing California for the crown.

Five hundred miles to the east, where the Spaniards had begun settlements, Fray Eusebio Francisco Kino, the indefatigable "Padre on Horseback," founded twenty-nine missions in Sonora and "Arizona." Between 1687 and 1711, he ventured over great stretches of land to reach the Colorado River. Kino constantly pressured his superiors to establish missions in the Baja California peninsula by 1697. The Jesuits received complete control of the region and the right to seek special private funding for the undertaking.

Juan María de Salvatierra and the Ugarte brothers were among the Jesuits who founded fourteen missions in Baja California in spite of recalcitrant natives, lack of rainfall, and an impossible geography made up of deserts and rugged mountains.

As early as 1708, King Philip V of Spain had ordered a new port on the Pacific, but his order was never carried out. Julio de Oliban, a member of the Audencia de Guadalajara had proposed to the king that there be founded a settlement on San Diego Bay, a place he called "capacious, pleasant, and well-situated"; the king spoke of settling the region "before the enemies of [his] crown occup[ied] it."

Above Left: On the evening of November 4, 1775, Diegueño Indians attacked Mission San Diego de Alcalá. The simple structure was readily destroyed, and Father Luis Jayme became the first Franciscan to meet martyrdom at Indian hands. Survivors of the attack withdrew to the presidio, six miles west. Within a year the padres had begun to rebuild a new mission at the site of Nipaguay, where the earlier church had been. Above Right: A Cahuilla olla, or water jug.

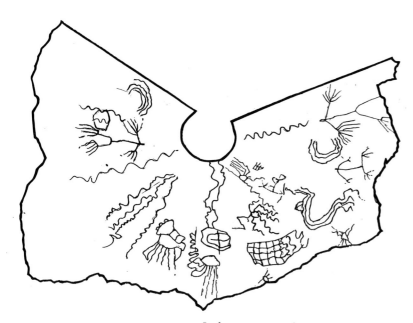

Indian pictographs are combined in a drawing by A. Welts, an archaeologist and historian. The symbols are not always decipherable; however, experts have determined that some of them refer to religious and mythical subjects.

The Spanish galleons of 1732, crossing the Pacific and following the coastline to return to ports in Mexico, had orders to unite at San Diego Bay, and although they moved toward the entrance to the harbor, bad weather prevented them from entering.

In 1734, a Manila galleon dropped anchor at Cape San Lucas in Lower California. The ship's captain, in violation of Spanish maritime regulations which prohibited stops on voyages from the Philippines and the Orient, took refuge in the harbor, and the Jesuits came to the aid of the exhausted crew.

In that year some Lower California Indians rebelled, and martyred two priests. Sigismundo Taraval, S.J., wrote in *The Indian Uprising in Lower California, 1734–1737*, the uprising had been brought about by the imposition of a rule which deprived the Indians of some of their customs, including the one which allowed plural marriages.

Miguel Venegas, a Jesuit, followed the remarkable men who labored to conquer the barren and inhospitable peninsula, and his work, published in Spanish in 1758, related *The Natural and Civil History of Lower California.*

By this time Spanish sailors and soldiers had explored and occupied large portions of Mexico, Latin America, and the Pacific. Spain had become a world power weakened by wars at home and showed concern with the turn of events in North America, where the British, French, and Dutch had challenged the Spanish right to dominate the New World. As other nations searched for furs and natural resources for wealth, Spain no longer had the strength to carry out the exploitation.

The Russian Vitus Bering with the vessels *St. Peter* and *St. Paul* explored from Kamchatka and the Aleutians; Spain had already turned inward to present day New Mexico and Texas. She launched troops and missionaries into that field.

The Britisher Captain James Cook undertook three major voyages from 1768 – 1771, 1772 – 1775, and in 1776 to find the "Northwest Passage" to the Indies through or around North America.

Correspondence from Spain warned José de Gálvez, the *visitador-general* and special deputy of the King of Spain, of possible Russian interest in California. Gálvez used that warning to strengthen his own argument to advance into Alta California. He also rationalized that the threat of the English, Dutch, and French intrusions would support his plans.

The Russian threat had been overstated. Catherine the Great faced innumerable problems at home and elsewhere in a war with Turkey.

A more imminent danger lay in Britain's Hudson Bay Colony, the great fur-trapping fraternity which had extended its commerce into the Pacific Northwest. The Gálvez plan to occupy Monterey and San Diego began to take shape as early as 1765.

When the kings of Spain, France, and Portugal became convinced that the Jesuits had power and wealth (which they had not) and hidden assets in various parts of the world, including a hoard of gold and pearls at the "Lost Mission of Santa Ysabel" (which proved nonexistent), the King of Spain ordered them expelled from all the Spanish dominions. In 1767 the Jesuits left Lower California under guard, and the Franciscans entered the California missionary field.

The Spanish Crown concluded that her small army could not continue expansive warfare in the New World and retreated to a less aggressive position: as humans with souls to be saved, natives could become baptized Christians, be protected, and have certain rights as citizens of Spain. To carry out this idea the Spaniards used the trinity of the *misión* as a frontier institution, the *presidio* or fort which sometimes evolved into a village, and the *pueblo* or town.

Above Left: This Diegueño Indian woman displayed her child in a pack normally worn on the mother's back. Indian women wore colorful, cotton clothing often traded or purchased from the Mexican population. Above: The two photographs depict examples of the tule structures which the Indians built for summer living. The lower photograph was taken at Pala, where for some years the cross and the mission bells represented Christianity for these peoples.

Age of Discovery

23

Aboard the galleon Golden Hinde, *Sir Francis Drake searched for the mythical Northwest Passage to the Indies in 1579. This illustration was drawn by Raymond Aker, an authority on sixteenth-century ships, navigation, cartography, and hydrology.*

José de Gálvez's plan, hammered out at a meeting in 1768, launched the Sacred Expedition to occupy Alta or Upper California. The professionals who served as the *junta* were Antonio Faveau de Quesada, Professor of Mathematics in the Manila Galleon Service; Miguel Costansó, one of the two engineer cartographers; Vicente Vila, Chief Pilot of the Department of San Blas; and Don Manual Rivero Cordero, officer in charge of construction at San Blas. Gálvez presided over the council.

He commanded that not only should the several parts of the expedition rendezvous in San Diego, but that "one of the most interesting objectives of this expedition should be to explore, and settle if it be possible, the port of San Diego."

Two expeditions moved northward through the Lower California peninsula, and by September 1768 the first land division under Captain Fernando Rivera y Moncada with Fray Juan Crespi as chaplain had left Velicatá, the newest mission and the only one founded by the Franciscans in Lower California.

The second land expedition, led by the military commander of the expedition and governor of Lower California, Gaspar de Portolá, and by Fray Junípero Serra, *presidente* or superior of the missions, left from Loreto. With the two parties were *soldados de cuera* (leather-jacket soldiers), cuirassiers, and Christianized Indians from the Baja California missions.

Whether the expeditions meant to found a mission and *presidio* at San Diego is still moot; what is known is that they were to establish stations along the way to Monterey, one of which became San Diego.

The *San Carlos* and the *San Antonio* left Cabo San Lucas. The *San Antonio* arrived first on April 11, 1769 and cast anchor near Punta de Guijarros or Ballast Point. Half of the crew of the vessel had come down with scurvy or other dietary-deficiency diseases, and many of the crew had died. Only seven men were able to work. Even Captain Juan Perez and two Franciscans, Juan Vizcaíno and Francisco Gómez, could scarcely walk.

The *San Carlos,* under Captain Vicente Vilá with Fray Fernando Parrón aboard, had left before the other vessel, but a series of unfortunate events kept her from arriving in San Diego until April 29, 1769.

Vilá wrote, "I discovered the packet *San Antonio* anchored at Punta de Guijarros. We broke out our colors. She broke out hers and fired one gun to call in her launch which was ashore." Vilá learned that the crew of the *San Antonio* was incapacitated, and the *San Carlos* had had her own troubles with an unhealthy crew, which lacked fresh food and sufficient medicines. The ailing surgeon, Pedro Prat, could do little to help. After hearing Holy Mass on board, those who were strong enough to do so went ashore on May 3, 1769, to bury the dead, to explore the country, and to search for drinking water.

At Santa Cruz on May 10, 1769, on the coast of Sonora, by orders of José de Gálvez the *San José* was blessed, and Fray Francisco Palóu sang High Mass aboard her before a beautiful image of the Virgin. During this Holy Sacrifice, Don José de Gálvez, to the edification of all, received Holy Communion. After the divine services he formally named the new ship in honor of his most holy patriarch, Saint Joseph.

Three months later this ship laden with religious goods and military arms reappeared as a ghost at a port in Sonora, having been buffeted by winds and unable to sail around the cape.

Reprovisioned she set sail but was never seen again. The loss of the *San José* would soon cause great uncertainty at San Diego about the success of the expedition, and her absence caused grave privation at that port. Gone were the foodstuffs: dried meat, fish, figs, raisins, brandy, wine, and clothing for the Alta California Indians.

Lost were seven cannons including three large twelve-pound artillery bronze cannons mounted on their carriages, and two small eight-pound swivel guns. Among the items in the ship's chapel were a communion table, a statue of Holy Christ, priest's vestments, chalices, and other religious objects intended for California missions, including bells for a church tower and coins.

Livestock on board intended for Alta California were ewes, rams, hens, and roosters. The ship's inventory included earthenware jars from Guadalajara, China plates, *chocolateros* (cups), metal table service, and *metates y manos.*

Don José de Gálvez outfitted the expeditions in 1796 which developed the first settlements in Upper California. He is generally known as the founder of California.

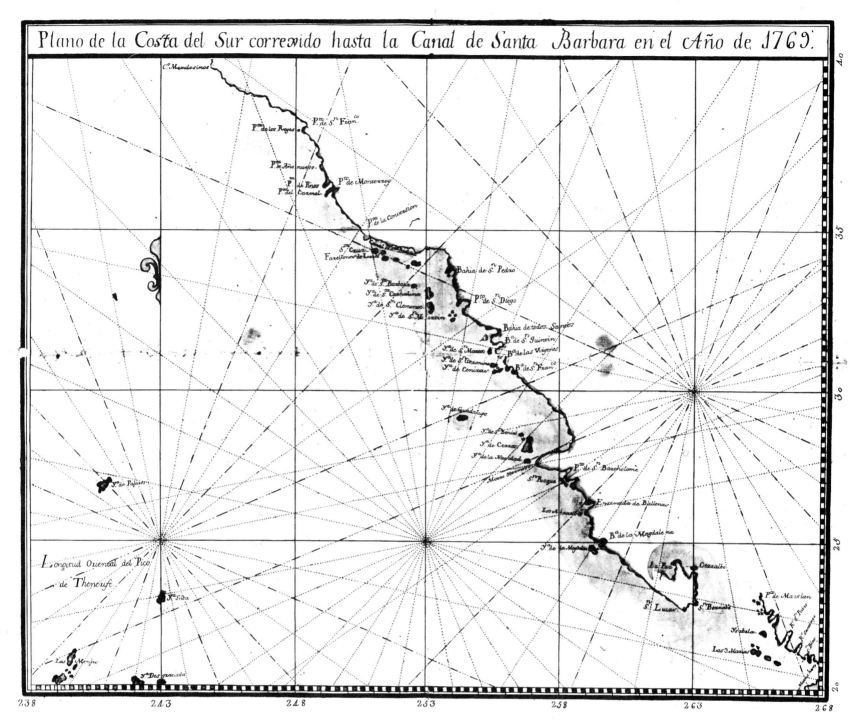

This is the first map showing observations by the Portolá Expedition, drawn by Jorge Storace, sailing master on the San Carlos in 1769. The map of the California coast, "corrected up to the Santa Barbara Channel," appeared in The Costansó Narrative of the Portolá Expedition, *the first chronicle of the Spanish conquest of Alta California. Miguel Cos-* tansó was an engineer who accompanied the Sacred Expedition to California.

San Diego
An Illustrated History

26

OTICIOSO EL ALTO GO-
vierno de España de las repeti-
das Tentativas de una Nacion
Extrangera fobre las Coftas
Septentrionales de la California, con miras nada favorables
á la Monarquia, y á fus Interefes, mandó el
REY al Marqués de Croix, fu Virrey, y Ca-
pitan General en la Nueva España diefe efi-
cazes Providencias para refguardar parte de
fus Dominios de toda Invasion, é Infulto.

The ship's crew, which included the captain, first and second pilots, a missionary, twenty-five sailors, one cook, and two servants, was lost at sea.

At San Diego on May 10, those few able seamen went ashore to begin building living quarters, determining to build on a "hillock close by the beach and a cannon shot from the packets." The next day a launch went ashore with two cannons and a supply of muskets and bullets. Jerked beef to be used for soup and hardtack went first for the sick. The outlook for survival dimmed as one by one the crew members continued to die aboard ship.

Four days later, on a Sunday afternoon of May 14, the first land expedition led by Rivera Moncada arrived at the camp near the San Diego River. Fray Juan Crespi wrote:

. . . we found a general hospital erected for the men of both vessels and for twenty-five volunteer soldiers from the *San Carlos.* Until now, twenty-three sailors have died. Nearly all the survivors of the sea expeditions are suffering very much from scurvy. Very few can keep on their feet. Only by a miracle will most of them be able to escape with their lives.

Above Left: The sixteenth-century Spanish breastplate is among a collection at the Los Angeles County Museum of Natural History. While European explorers came to the New World fully armored, the extreme heat of the southwestern desert edged out use of the clumsy apparatus. Top: The first page of Miguel Costansó's historical diary, reportedly published in Mexico in 1770. Above: The cartridge box, dated approximately 1790, is simply a block of wood with holes bored in it to hold paper cartridges.

Age of Discovery

DIARIO HISTORICO
DE LOS VIAGES DE MAR, Y TIERRA
HECHOS AL NORTE DE LA CALIFORNIA
DE ORDEN
DEL EXCELENTISSIMO SEÑOR
MARQUES DE CROIX,
Virrey, Governador, y Capitan General de la Nueva España:
Y POR DIRECCION
DEL ILLUSTRISSIMO SEÑOR
D.JOSEPH DE GALVEZ,
Del Consejo, y Camara de S. M. en el Supremo de Indias, Intendente de Exercito, Visitador General de este Reyno.

Top Left: Primarily a war vessel, this version of the English corvette was employed as a supply carrier along the California coast from 1790 to 1840. Top Right: The Jodocus Hondius map shows the routes of the Drake and Cavendish voyages. Above: The title page from the first printing of Costansó's diary. The diary, housed in the Los Angeles Public Library, was published in 1970.

San Diego
An Illustrated History

28

In 1734, a Manila galleon dropped anchor at Cape San Lucas in Lower California. The ship's captain, in violation of Spanish maritime regulations which prohibited stops on voyages from the Philippines and the Orient, took refuge in the harbor, and the Jesuits came to the aid of the men who had exhausted their food and water.

In that year some Lower California Indians rebelled, and martyred two priests. Sigismundo Taraval, S.J., wrote in *The Indian Uprising in Lower California, 1734 – 1737,* the uprising had been brought about by the imposition of a rule which deprived the Indians of some of their customs, including the one which allowed plural marriages.

Miguel Venegas, a Jesuit, followed the remarkable men who labored to conquer the barren and inhospitable peninsula, and his work, published in Spanish in 1758, related *The Natural and Civil History of Lower California.*

The second land expedition arrived at San Diego on June 29, 1769, as Sergeant José Francisco Ortega led the reconnoitering party several days ahead of the main party.

Don Gaspar de Portolá and Junípero Serra arrived on Saturday July 1, 1769. Some 119 people, the survivors of the Sacred Expedition, including the ill, celebrated a solemn High Mass on July 2, a Sunday and the Feast of the Visitation of the Blessed Virgin Mary. The Mass was offered up to Almighty God in honor of St. Joseph. On July 3, Serra wrote to Father Palóu that all but two men of the *San Carlos* had passed away.

Near the mouth of Mission Bay, "just two musket shots" from the harbor of San Diego, these southern Europeans built structures of tule and brush to found the "Birthplace of California."

On the morning of July 16, 1769, a High Mass was said by the Franciscan Junípero Serra. He noted the day as a very memorable one because five centuries earlier under the same diurnal sign, Spanish forces had defeated the Mohammedans at Las Nava de Tolosa.

Above: Through the years, explorers, the military, and cattle- and sheepherders have trampled the prehistoric trails lacing the Laguna, Cuyamaca, and other back mountain ranges. These ancient roadways, then as now, followed the easiest route—the line of least resistance.

Top Right: Dr. James R. Moriarty and students from the University of San Diego excavated at Del Mar where evidence of prehistoric man was first discovered during the 1920s. Proximity to the shoreline must have been as attractive to prehistoric people as it was to the students conducting the field archaeology.

Above: One-and-a-half-foot bunkers were preserved for detailed profiling of the remaining stratum.

The record book of the mission contains entries showing the zeal of the Spaniards to assist the padres in erecting the church.

Estevan Martinez, captain of the San Carlos, used cedar from his vessel to make doors and an altar table. Juan de Ayala, commander of the frigate San Diego, built three chairs for the church out of a chunk of cypress. Vessels arriving

from Mexico, China, and the Philippines also contributed to the mission's architecture.

CHAPTER 2

The Far Western Frontier

ALREADY DON PEDRO FAGES, Miguel Costansó, and the Franciscans, Fray Juan Crespi and Fray Juan Gonzalez Vizcaíno, had begun to explore Mission Valley along the San Diego River, finding a site close to the Nipaguay *rancheria* that would become the location of the first Franciscan mission in California.

Their *diarios* explained that the natives used the environment to their advantage by hunting certain types of pheasant, quail, and hawk. Archaeologists have identified bone material found in Indian campsites as that of game now extinct in this region. The Indians gathered wild berries, roots, and greens in the river valleys. At the edge of the surf they harvested seafoods and caught flounder, bonito, and halibut.

Remaining fragments of seashell, plain brown pottery sherds, and rock circles reveal to archaeologists the location and nature of a primitive people.

The party met Indians armed with bows and arrows. The natives waved white cloths signaling they wanted to parley. Debilitated by their march from Lower California, the Spaniards did all they could to hide their weakness. Gestures of peace brought the two parties together, and after receiving glass, beads, ribbons, and baubles, the natives led the way to their *rancheria*. There, thirty to

Top: The home of Alcalde Juan Maria Marron was one of the few adobe structures still maintained at the foot of presidio hill in 1874, when this photograph was taken. Above: This 1782 map of the port figured as one of the key guides for the Treaty of Guadalupe Hidalgo.

San Diego
An Illustrated History

32

forty families lived in a protective enclosure where they indicated they could fortify themselves.

Serra wrote on July 3, 1769 that the Spaniards had met with no hostility. They were glad they had goods to share with the gentiles.

The governor, Don Gaspar de Portalá, set out for Monterey, taking nearly every man who could travel, leaving Father Serra with the invalids and a few soldiers. The *San Antonio* sailed for San Blas, a port on the coast of Sonora, with a few men to obtain more food and supplies.

In August 1769, shortly after the force went out to Monterey, there remained on the *presidio* hill a small number of leather-jacket soldiers and Catalonian Volunteers, all sick or disabled. The Indians struck the camp. Father Vizcaíno, Chacon, a blacksmith from Guadalajara, and two other men were wounded; a servant was killed. First driven off, the Indians soon came near to get help for their wounded.

Nothing had been heard from the governor until his party reappeared on January 24, 1770. In the interim all personnel had expected that either the *San José* or the *San Antonio* would return with provisions. There had been no inkling that the *San José* would never reach San Diego.

Supplies had run short, and when Portolá resolved not to lose any more men, he decided to give up San Diego. Serra, Lieutenant Pedro Fages, and Costansó struck a bargain with the governor to hold on until March 19, the Feast of St. Joseph; if by that day relief had not come, they would then retreat southward and abandon Alta California.

On the morning of March 19, 1770, the Feast of St. Joseph was celebrated, and all preparations to leave had been completed

when Serra, who had been watching the ocean, saw a ship pass the entrance to the harbor. Four days later the *San Antonio* arrived.

The mission was established and by December 1774, priests, artisans, and Indians had constructed some buildings, including a palisade roofed with tule. Missionaries Luis Jayme and Vicente Fuster baptized Indians, encouraged their work, and helped them to grow crops and herd cattle in the valley.

During the night of November 4, 1775, about 800 well-armed warriors raided the mission. Simultaneously another party attacked the *presidio*. Indians overpowered the soldiers at the mission, burned and destroyed the delicate mission structures, carried off religious objects, and martyred Father Jayme.

The Spaniards who survived retreated to the *presidio*, but in that same year they returned to Nipaguay and built a second church of adobe blocks with a mud-covered, thatched roof that would not catch fire. By 1780 the padres had built a third church; this one, of adobe and timber, was more spacious and substantial. It was blessed in 1781, and most of the structure lasted until 1808.

Lieutenant Fages ordered buildings constructed at the site, the Indian village of Cosoy, but the Spaniards lived on the brink of disaster. Not until August 1772 did supply vessels arrive to end the period of starvation. A fortified wall surrounded the little town. By 1774 the padres left the place now officially called the Royal Presidio of San Diego and moved six miles east in Mission Valley to Nipaguay.

As early as March 1778, Indians again planned to attack the mission and *presidio*. The soldiers learned of the plots and went into the *rancherías* to dole out punishment.

Now on a more regular basis the packet boats arrived to supplement the stores and supplies. On March 16, 1778, the *San Car-*

Above Left: On the eastern slope of the Laguna Mountains, the community of Vallecito proved a valuable watering hole and campsite for Indians and, later, the Boundary Survey Commission when traveling between San Diego and Yuma. John Russell Bartlett, Boundary Survey Commissioner, produced an enormous number of watercolors, such as this one, and pen and ink sketches of significant places, events and people en route. Above: The stagecoach station at Vallecito, between San Diego and Yuma, was an important stop for the Butterfield Overland Mail Company line. Here the line changed drivers and horses while passengers ate and took fresh water from the springs before the climb over the Laguna Mountains to the coast. Abbott and Downing of Concord, New Hampshire, built the finest of these coaches which averaged about five miles an hour.

Far Western Frontier

The erection of a high, adobe wall to contain the mission and several outer structures was part of an early reconstruction phase ending in 1785. Yet the padres perennially seemed faced with the cost of reconstruction. In the 1800s two damaging earthquakes were followed by a somewhat disorderly army occupation of the site. The mission fell into ruins before 1850.

San Diego
An Illustrated History

34

los, under command of First Pilot Don José Camacho, arrived off Point Loma and took on water. Camacho then sent some men to the *presidio* for help to unload the vessel. The *San Carlos* had brought beans, hard tack, dried fish, chile, flour, cheese, and other dried foods. She also carried kitchen utensils, weapons, and necessities to sustain the population.

Many adventurous souls left Culiacan, Alamos, or Tubac on the Mexican mainland and traveled overland to the Spanish coastal port of San Diego. What brought these people to traverse deserts and a thousand miles through a *tierra incognita* to California? Why had they wished to start life over again on a new frontier? Had they dreamt of owning land or of finding wealth? Where the magnet had once been fanciful notions, the pull now seemed to be the human need to make a new life.

The San Diego *presidio* families were middle- and lower-class settlers from Mexico and Lower California with Mestizos (Span-

ish and Indian) probably making up the largest group. They lived inside the walled city around the brush chapel. News from the outside world came by vessel, but more often mail couriers on horseback traveled from the *presidio* at Loreto in Lower California as far north as Monterey every week or two.

Between 1800 and 1828 ships from the major nations of the world visited San Diego Harbor, including some from Russia, France, Spain, and the Sandwich (Hawaiian) Islands.

In 1803, Richard J. Cleveland and William Shaler in the *Lelia Byrd* exchanged shots with the small garrison located at Punta de Guijarros, an event sometimes affectionately referred to as the "Battle of San Diego."

Before 1810, the vessels carried the standard buttons, beads, bangles, and baubles; after that a typical cargo included wool and cotton clothing, axes, gunpowder, muskets, shot, bar lead, hardware, pots and kettles, sugar, molasses, hogsheads and kegs of rice, bars of iron, scissors, butcher knives, looking glasses, needles, pea jackets, and stockings. In exchange they took sea-otter skins, beaver, raccoon, wildcat, land-otter, badger, fox, mink, martin, and muskrat coats.

Mission San Diego do Alcalá fell into ruin with age and use. In the earthquake of December 31, 1812 the fourth church while under construction suffered structural damage. Fray Fernando Martín and Fray José Sánchez concluded that to brace the church against future quakes, flared wings could be added to the facade as buttresses against the tremors which rolled on a north-south axis. The blessing ceremonies signaled the completion of construction on November 12, 1813.

Above Left: The drawing depicts a member of the Voluntarios de Cataluña, *a regiment organized in Spain. In 1767 the First Battalion of the Second Regiment sailed for Mexico and served against the Apaches on the Sonora and Baja frontiers. Middle: The Serra Cross on presidio hill was built with tile and brick removed from the site of the Royal Presidio. This photograph, taken in 1917, shows the area before it was relandscaped and donated to the city as a park by George White Marston. Above Right: Although the subject of the John Russell Bartlett sketch is a Diegueño Indian, the hairstyle and features resemble those of a Mexican.*

Far Western Frontier

Pio Pico was the last Mexican governor of California, serving his final term from 1842 through 1845. In his later years he lost much of his wealth while struggling to compete with American businessmen.

At Nipaguay in 1813 the padres built an impressive dam and irrigation system for their crops and to water cattle which grazed over the large grants of land given to the missions. By the time of the Mexican War, the entire site had fallen into ruin.

Inside the walls at the *presidio* of San Diego, a city of sorts arose. Artisans, blacksmiths, leather makers, and soldiers and their families all built houses about the chapel. The port was under the command of Captain Francisco María Ruiz who was stationed there from 1806 to 1827.

The settlers, knowing little about farming, wore out the soil; their cattle overgrazed valley forage. One year they watched their crops dry up from lack of rainfall and the next gazed in dismay when their crops floated into San Diego Bay during a flood.

Presidio life seemed little touched by the outside world except when villages received a fright such as in 1818, when they heard that Hipolite Bouchard, a Frenchman who had joined the navy of the United Provinces of the Rio de la Plata (later the Argentine Republic) headed his warship for San Diego. He had been attacking Spanish shipping at Monterey and San Juan Capistrano. His vessel the *Argentina,* a heavily armed frigate of 671 tons burden, mounted 34 guns, with a crew of 450 sailors and 150 soldiers. No wonder the fear of the San Diegans and their relief as the vessel sailed past the harbor entrance.

By 1820 this walled city had a population of only 450 persons, with half that number military-related. The buildings deteriorated, the hillsides, timber, and resources fell prey to need. When heavy rains came, water rolled down the barren slopes and over the flood plain which would become the location of San Diego's second city, "Old Town."

In *Life in California Before the Conquest,* Alfred Robinson wrote of seeing governor José María Echeandía's house located in the center of the walled village, on a hill to command a view of the sea. Below the hill by 1821, stood some thirty homes mostly occupied by retired veterans. George Vancouver told of the retired soldiers, principally old Spanish or Creole men who had been given land as a reward for long service. They had selected patches of land to cultivate crops away from the cramped quarters of the fort. Here they could build their homes, farm, and plant orchards. In the fall of that year the San Diego river began to divert itself so that part of the river flowed past Old Town and into San Diego Bay; the rest continued to the ocean. While Old Town became the key location south of Los Angeles, outlying areas also reflected important aspects of California life.

In the heyday of ranches, cattle were grown for food, but a trade in hides or "California banknotes," as they came to be called, grew and an export business began. Boston ships had opened up the market in hides with the United States. The first hide ships

from Boston arrived in San Diego in 1825, and in 1829, the first of the hide houses was built at La Playa for the *Brookline.*

Inside Ballast Point crews from the ship worked on the beach; Kanakas, Frenchmen, and Britishers cleaned the fresh hides, scrubbing them with clear white sand and curing them in brine. In his book *Lewey and I . . .,* William H. Thomes tells of life on the beach where the crews lived in barnlike hide houses, each named for a ship they represented. The vessels traded Yankee goods: pottery, patent medicines, hardware, perfumes, and furniture were exchanged for wine, *aguardiente* (intoxicant), tallow, and hides.

The growing number of foreigners in California remained in the minds of the politicos, especially Echeandía, whose paranoia was reinforced by his keeping track of such persons through annual listings. He kept circulating a document of procedures for foreigners who wanted to become Mexican citizens.

Mountain man Jedediah Smith came to do business on December 23, 1826. On Christmas Day, Governor José María Echeandía refused Smith a license to trap and advised him to keep moving.

Trappers Sylvester Pattie and son, James Ohio Pattie, with six other trappers had come into the country without a license, according to Echeandía, and crossed the country in contradiction to laws cited by the governor.

Doña Juanita Machado Alípaz de Wrightington surveyed Old Town from her porch in this 1895 photograph. One of the daughters of Corporal Juan Machado, she first married the patriot Damasio Alípaz, who was killed while fighting in Sonora, and later Thomas Wrightington, a ship's captain from Massachusetts.

Far Western Frontier

37

Above: Joseph Francis Snook was an English mariner on the Mexican coast who married Maria Antonia Alvardo in 1837. He became grantee of the San Bernardo Rancho. Archaeologists from San Diego State University recently discovered his grave in the pre-sidio chapel. Above Right: Juan Bandini, a native of Peru and leader of the Old Town community from the 1820s until his death in 1859, had a penchant for keeping politicians honest, even in the face of a revolution. During the Mexican period, he recognized the distinct advantages of California's acquisition by the United States. This picture, with his daughter Margarita, was taken from a daguerreotype about 1851.

Jailed at the *presidio,* Sylvester died. How James Ohio Pattie came to be released remains a mystery, although a book by the Reverend Timothy Flint provides an exaggerated tale of Pattie vaccinating 22,000 Californians against smallpox, when in fact, *difuntos* (death records) for those years do not reflect smallpox deaths in great numbers. But, of such are myths spawned and heros born.

As Old Town took shape about 1828, inhabitants did develop relationships with foreigners despite a distrust of outsiders. The families Machado, Pico, Alvarado, Estudillo, and Bandini stayed closely knit. Into their midst came the likes of Alfonso Monarde of Italy, Peter Weldon from the States, Horatio Nelson Hartnell from Great Britain, and John Tierney from Ireland. The Kanakas and the Scotsman on the beach, the Frenchman Lewey and the Britisher Saleden on the ranch contributed to the international flavor of the port. Swearing allegiance to the Mexican government and being baptized in the Catholic faith, the national church, these men were permitted citizenship, and perhaps marriage with ladies of the *gente de razon.*

The village grew around a rectangular *placita* unlike the spoked wheels of Tucson, El Paso, or Los Angeles. Enveloping the Old Town plaza stood businesses and residences. The square became a central marketplace loaded with strings of chili, grain, fruits, *panoche,* buckets of figs, trays of tamales, and cactus fruit; Indians and Mexicans carted hides, wool, wood, and mocking birds

in bamboo cages. Periodically a circus came to town, and in November 1869, for three days Old Towners saw Lee and Ryland's Circus. The Paris Exposition Circus included, "The Learned Buffalo," "Juggler of Japan," "The Donovan Brothers," "The Menage of the Horse," and "Ala Pasha and Other Acts."

When Richard Henry Dana arrived in 1834 he wrote:

. . . the first place we went to was the old ruinous *presidio* which stands on a rising ground near the village which it overlooks. . . . The small settlement lay directly below the fort, composed of about forty dark brown looking huts or houses and two larger ones. . . .

The Old Town settlement now had enough people to seek local government, and regulations allowed a community of 432 people to have a mayor, four councilmen, and a city attorney.

The *comandante* of the *presidio*, Santiago Arguello, had been its one-man rule. When the time came he led the drive to collect signatures to replace himself with a city government. An election held in December 1834, chose Juan María Osuna the first *alcalde* (mayor). The *ayuntamiento* (town council) considered requests for land, support of schools, disposition of prisoners, and settlement of private debts. This body leased public lands, taxed the use of branding irons and the butchering of cattle, and levied taxes on entertainment, saloons, and stores.

Above Left: Although Old Town families were tightly knit, inter-marriages with foreigners were not uncommon. Guadalupe Machado (third from right) married Albert Smith and gathered with some of her ten siblings in this 1874 photograph. Her father, José Manuel Machado, had built five homes around the plaza, including this one on San Diego Avenue, for his children. Above: Henry Fitch, a Boston seaman, went so far as to become a Mexican citizen when he married Josefa Carrillo in 1827. He served San Diego in various governmental positions.

Above: Major shipping companies established depots, such as this one at seaside, for the curing of cowhides delivered from nearby missions and ranches. The busy depots, the first of which was built in 1829, prepared as many as forty thousand hides at one time for shipment. Above Right: The diorama portraying the Battle of San Pasqual on December 6, 1846, is an excellent representation of the bloody conflict between General Stephen Watts Kearny, commanding an army regiment, and the mounted lancers of Andrés Pico. The fierce battle revealed the skills of the hard-riding Californios to the U.S. Army. The war ended a month later with the surrender of the Mexican troopers on January 13, 1847.

In its first action the council issued a decree having to do with the "preservation of forests" and prohibiting the export of timber. Having already stripped adjacent hillsides of forestation and experiencing the aftermath of heavy rains, the townspeople began to grasp the meaning of conservationism.

San Diego grew out of the mission holdings. However, in August 1833, the Mexican government passed the acts of secularization which stripped thousands of acres of land from the missions. Soon the secular leaders took over and built up land holdings of California families.

The Indians, removed from the protection of the church, had not been prepared to go out on their own, but had learned to work with *rancheros* rounding up the thousands of cattle held by the missions. Now on land grants, Indians and Mexicans worked side by side during the roundups, the brandings, and the drives.

At a time when the Indians thought the Californios to be militarily weak and insufficiently armed, they attacked at various points in the back country. In 1835, Indians, probably Cahuilla, threatened to attack Santa Ysabel. A particularly bad year came in 1836, with every *ranchero* reporting robberies which were blamed on the Indians. The population at San Luis Rey Mission fled as the attacks intensified. When citizens asked the soldiers to go out on patrol, the soldiers responded that they had not been paid for three years.

Indians lived on the perimeter of Old Town and in *rancherías* along the bay and beach areas. Special local laws circumscribed their conduct. But the council made special efforts to protect the Indians. For another decade rumors of imminent attack plagued Old Towners, as Indians threatened to raid the pueblo as a way to gain independence.

The local laws of 1835 mirrored the social and moral attitudes of the times. *Bandos* or "decrees" prohibited cattle inside the city

limits, and streets not swept clean brought fines to impress property owners with concepts of health standards.

The mayor, Enrique Fitch, prohibited the carrying of weapons in the *pueblo*. No person could stay in the town without a means of support. A *bando* of six articles prohibited gambling; drunks received a two day sentence to the work gang. The council, in that way, totally eliminated vagrancy by mandatory work sentences.

In February, 1835, a Secularization Commission wanted to establish a school to continue the teaching of youth but ordered that the teacher could not be a stranger or foreigner.

Just before Christmas, 1835, Mayor Fitch asked the *Juez de Paz* (Justice of the Peace) for a separation from his wife for she had gambled away $1,000. The separation was temporarily ordered. She admitted to her indiscretions, begged forgiveness, and promised to deport herself properly.

In 1837, Juan Bandini conspired to replace Juan Bautista Alvarado, governor of the California province. Carlos Antonio Carrillo of San Diego had supposedly been appointed by the Mexican government to replace Alvarado. Southern Californians supported Carrillo, but Northern Californians did not. Carrillo led a small army to skirmish with his adversaries in Los Angeles but retreated to San Diego for help. Bandini brought together a small force to do battle with Alvarado at Oceanside. The two governors waged a verbal battle and Carrillo ended up with the office.

By 1845, with a large number of foreigners on the Pacific Coast, officials expected confrontation from within. Pio Pico, then governor, predicted the end of Mexican California and gave away thousands of square miles of California land to his relatives, friends, and himself.

War broke out between Mexico and the United States; on July 30, 1846, the American twenty-two gun corvette *Cyane* sailed into San Diego harbor. Captained by Samuel F. DuPont, the ves-

Top: Men donned calzoneras, *or long pants, and women lacy* mantillas *for the festive* fandangos *on frontier ranches in the 1840s. Above: Painted floral and leaf designs decorate this working saddle, reflecting the pride of the* ranchero *in his equipment. The saddle dates to 1855.*

Far Western Frontier

41

Student archaeologists painstakingly brush and scrape the soil searching for clues about man's past. The documentary evidence of life in California two-hundred or more years ago, however well written by the Spaniards, does not reveal data of day-to-day activities. Interdisciplinary studies enable students of photography, cartography, illustration, biology, history, and architecture to work together.

sel anchored. Aboard were the pathmarker John C. Frèmont, Kit Carson, the scout Alex Godey, and several Delaware Indians. Lieutenant Stephen C. Rowan of the United States Navy and Marine Corps and Lieutenant William A. T. Maddox led sailors and marines ashore to raise the U.S. flag in Old Town. DuPont took over a fort the Mexicans had built on *presidio* hill, renaming it appropriately for himself.

Not all Mexicans wanted government by the United States. Forces rendezvoused in the back country, and since only a few Americans remained in San Diego, the Mexicans retook the town. The Mexican flag flew over the Old Town plaza again.

In November 1846, Commodore Robert F. Stockton returned on the U.S.S. *Congress*, put 100 men ashore, drove the Californios off *presidio* hill, changed the name from DuPont to Fort Stockton, posted a garrison, and settled the *pueblo* down—all within a matter of hours.

The commodore learned that General Stephen Watts Kearny, who had left New Mexico to support the conquest, approached San Diego with his "Army of the West." Kearny's men had already crossed the desert, abandoned their artillery, and the troops had arrived exhausted.

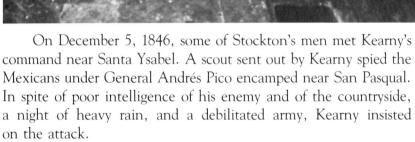

On December 5, 1846, some of Stockton's men met Kearny's command near Santa Ysabel. A scout sent out by Kearny spied the Mexicans under General Andrés Pico encamped near San Pasqual. In spite of poor intelligence of his enemy and of the countryside, a night of heavy rain, and a debilitated army, Kearny insisted on the attack.

Early the next morning before the fog had lifted, he sent out an advanced detachment which failed to wait for the main force. The well-mounted Mexicans with lances aligned struck first. Eighteen Americans were killed and thirteen wounded. Kearny lost one fifth of his command. The skilled horsemen encircled the soldiers on Mule Hill.

That night General Kearny dispatched Kit Carson, Edward F. Beale, and a Delaware scout. They walked barefoot and crawled over rocks and cactus so as to make no sound. The three men reached San Diego to get the needed reinforcements. Four days later 250 marines and sailors arrived at the scene, and Pico's lancers pulled away.

Frémont took his volunteers to Los Angeles where on February 13, 1847, General Andrés Pico surrendered without gunfire.

Above Left: Perhaps the most exciting discovery by historians at the Royal Presidio was this altar and ambry in 1967, which for the first time conclusively proved the existence of a chapel at the presidio. Above: Ceramics recovered through archeological excavations at Mission San Diego reveal manufacture at Staffordshire, Stoke-on-Trent, in the nineteenth century.

Far Western Frontier

Between 1854 and 1860, the Robinson-Rose house on the west side of the Old Town Plaza served as headquarters for The San Diego Herald and the San Diego and Gila Railroad. Judge James W. Robinson, who headed the railroad, offered a portion of the building for a school in 1855 and a remaining section was occupied by the Masonic Lodge Number Thirty-Five. At the time this picture was taken in 1872, the saloon and restaurant sold Vicksburg Lager, Chicago beer and plug cut. The group shown here are the San Diego Guards, a militia company formed in May 1856. One of its members was later arrested in New Mexico as a spy for the Confederate States of America.

CHAPTER 3

Americans Arrive
A New Town Arises

WILLIAM H. EMORY SAW Old Town before the Mexican War had ended and in his *Notes of a Military Reconnaissance,* the entry of December 12, 1846, reads:

The town consists of a few adobe houses, two or three of which have only plank floors . . . the rain fell in torrents as we entered the town, and it was my singular fate here . . . to be quartered in . . . a miserable place of one room.

Word pictures such as Emory's conjure up bleak and unpromising images of the frontier village of San Diego. Soldiers, who often see the seamy side of life in their wartime adventures, also reported that the village offered little in the way of physical comfort or beauty. Journalists and writers, those trained to see beyond the superficial, described San Diego as run down.

There remain numerous pen and ink sketches of Old Town by soldier and civilian alike — drawings that reveal a much different portrait of the pueblo. They show the neat homes with their well-tended gardens which bordered the aligned streets. The homes belonged to the Machado, Aguirre, Estudillo, and Bandini families — a group that served as the center of the community for years. (Some of these structures still stand and today are part of Old Town State Historic Park.) John Russell Bartlett, the

Above: "California Lancer," illustrated by William H. Meyers in 1846, was published in the work Naval Sketches of the War in California. *While the plate is identified, "typical lancer of the Mexican troops that opposed the American naval forces in California," many of the Californios were not uniformed, nor did they display fancy trappings. Left: Captain Samuel Francis DuPont commanded the U.S.S.* Cyane *which took possession of San Diego in July 1846. Once the town was secured and the American flag hoisted, DuPont stayed at the Juan Bandini home, participating in the festivities and writing about the enthusiasm of the Mexicanos to have the Americans among them.*

Boundary Survey Commissioner, Henry Miller, artist of the 1850s, Cave Couts, military officer, and H.M.T. Powell, forty-niner, all drew early sketches of the town, portraying it as a first-class frontier town.

The village was neither magnificent nor insignificant. Here and there were a few pretentious adobe residences in the Spanish style. When the Americans began to arrive with prefabricated buildings which had been shipped around the horn, they built frame structures.

Old Town never wanted for political leaders or spokesmen: Osuna, Argüello, Alvarado, or Ruiz helped run the city. It had its businessmen, cattlemen, and ranchers: Stewart, Fitch, Pedrorena, and Altamirano. It had social functions at the homes of Bandini, Estudillo, and Serrano.

Organizations such as the Masons and the Veterans of the Mexican War met regularly at the Congress Hall or the Jolly Boy Saloon, and became legends in their own time.

But with all the bustle of a small Latin frontier community, proper and moral behavior was expected. Laws produced customs and social conduct which generally kept a lid on troublemakers.

On May 15, 1847, Enrique Fitch, the *alcalde*, published a *bando* which dealt with acceptable behavior for in-town In-

dians. The ten regulations included the order to patrol the streets every night so as to arrest all Indians or *gente de razon* who might be creating problems. Each person of Indian background would have to produce a document showing that he or she was engaged in some useful occupation. Drunkards would be punished, and Indian women without work or of scandalous occupation would be sentenced to sweep the streets and plaza for fifteen days. Other laws seem equally punitive.

According to regulations affecting Mexican citizens, cases involving gambling or drunkenness, horse stealing, tavern violations, and servants who did wrong all had to be submitted to the civil authorities for prosecution.

Bringing balance to a sometimes raucous frontier town was the Mormon Battalion led by Lieutenant Colonel Philip St. George Cooke who arrived in 1847 too late to fight in the war. The guide who brought the Mormons to the coast was Jean Baptiste Charbonneau, son of Sacajawea, the interpreter and guide for

Top: "The Fight at San Pasqual" by William H. Meyers, dated 1846. Above Left: This 1850 sketch by H.M.T. Powell shows Point Loma as seen from presidio hill. Above: In 1846 Robert Field Stockton assumed command of all American forces on the Pacific coast. Above Right: Lieutenant Colonel Philip St. George Cooke led the Mormon Battalion from Fort Leavenworth, Missouri, to San Diego at the time of the war with Mexico. The Mormons were issued to bring order to the frontier settlement.

Americans Arrive
A New Town Arises

Originally the home of Doña María Reyes Ybañes, this structure (no longer extant) and the home of Don Pio Pico, to the rear, marked an important corner in Old Town in the 1820s. When Señora Ybañes, the much-respected matriarch of the Estudillo family, passed away, the house became a general merchandise store, boardinghouse, and saloon. Today this area, which includes the Bazaar del Mundo (built in the 1930s and then called the Casa de Pico auto court), is part of Old Town State Historic Park.

the Lewis and Clark expedition. Later, while an Indian agent at San Luis Rey, he fought to ameliorate the inhumane treatment of the Indians in that area.

While in San Diego, the wife of Captain Jesse D. Hunter of the battalion, died in childbirth. Scheduled to leave, Hunter left his new son with Juana Machado, known to many as "La Beata," who raised him until his father could take the boy some years later.

Once in San Diego, the Mormons, who had experience in crafts, hired themselves out to the townspeople. They built a kiln to fire red bricks, dug wells, whitewashed buildings, and constructed a bakery.

Brevet Major Samuel Peter Heintzelman, who commanded units of the regular U.S. troops, wrote of life in Old Town saying that by the spring of 1849, most of the able-bodied civilians had gone to the Northern California gold fields, leaving the town deserted except for the women and children. However, by the time cold weather set in, the luckless miners had returned home.

On July 3, 1849, the brig *Caroline* dropped the members of the Mexican Boundary Survey Commission off at San Diego where they received considerable attention from the American Boundary Survey Commission. More than fifty civilians and commission members took part in a ceremony. The representatives of the two

nations were charged with surveying and recording the new international boundary line resulting from the war.

The Mexican commission was headed by General Pedro García Condé, former military commander of Chihuahua; his assistant, José Salazar Ylarregui, was the surveyor. Other representatives included Felipe de Iturbide, son of the emperor of Mexico. Felipe served as official interpreter and translator.

The two international commission teams tried to work together, but the gold rush in Northern California proved a temptation and crew members from both sides, like the civilians, deserted to go north. Members of the U.S. team wrote home of interesting events including a brawl in the public square at Old Town between a U.S. major and a lieutenant over the honor of another man's sweetheart.

Disputes between the teams over the precise boundaries to be drawn marred a most unusual survey. On July 14, 1851, the commissions deposited a record beneath a monument marking the initial point of boundary between the United States and Mexico.

Top: Whitewashed adobe structures, such as the one belonging to Alcalde Marron, were gradually replaced with Americanized frame dwellings. Above: In one of the earliest sketches of Old Town, William H. Emory accurately depicted proximity of the pueblo to the bay. Since this drawing in 1846, drainage, dredging, and other marine actions have altered the size, shape, and depth of San Diego Bay.

Americans Arrive
A New Town Arises

"The Last Day With the Wagons," drawn by John Mix Stanley in 1846, was published in Lieutenant William H. Emory's Notes of a Military Reconnaissance from Fort Leavenworth, Missouri, to San Diego in California including parts of Arkansas, Del Norte and Gila Rivers. *The lithograph reflects but one of the many trials experienced by troopers before they arrived in California to do battle in the Mexican War.*

On August 16, 1849, Governor Bennett Riley had returned the *ayuntamiento* to local government. The act to incorporate the City of San Diego passed March 27, 1850; the first government elected included a mayor and a council of five members.

Joshua Bean, brother of "Law West of the Pecos" Roy Bean, became the first mayor under the new system and he was sworn in on January 10, 1850.

The Mormons made some 40,000 bricks for the courthouse which was finished in 1847. This building served at various times as the town hall, the first Episcopal Church, and headquarters for the U.S. Army and the Boundary Survey Commission. It served as Colonel John Bankhead Magruder's law office, the sheriff's office, and the town marshall's office. The clerk of the San Diego Common Council had one room, the mayor another, and there was a one-room jail in this same place.

California was admitted to the Union on September 9, 1850, and the American government pledged to protect resident Mexican citizens in the "free enjoyment of their liberty, property, and religion," and to recognize their rights to land claimed by virtue of titles conforming to Spanish and Mexican regulations in force when they were issued.

San Diego County included all of Imperial County, most of Riverside and San Bernardino counties, and the east half of Inyo County. By 1907 the county had been reduced to its present size.

Bayard Taylor saw the harbor of San Diego in 1850 and thought it to be the finest on the Pacific except for Acapulco. In his book *El Dorado* he spoke of the hide houses at the landing place built at the foot of the hills just inside the bay, and of a fine road along the shore leading to the town of San Diego which was situated on a plain.

Top Left: Ysidora Bandini de Couts wielded considerable influence as one of the original settlers of Old Town. Top Right: Cave Johnson Couts maintained a wholesome image while standing trial as a gambler, swindler and murderer. His ability to draw resulted in the sketch (above) of Old Town.

Americans Arrive
A New Town Arises

51

On the beach were clustered a number of people and boats laden with passengers and freight waiting to board the ship headed for San Francisco. He described a number of men:

. . . lank and brown as is the ribbed sea . . . with long hair and beards, and faces from which the rigid expression of suffering was scarcely relaxed. They were the first of the overland emigrants by the Gila route, who had reached San Diego a few days before. Their clothes were in tatters, their boots in many cases replaced by moccasins.

By late 1849 the United States Army had begun to settle itself at Mission San Diego, at La Playa on Point Loma, and at Old Town. Major Samuel Peter Heintzelman issued a special order on June 19, 1850, restricting construction of buildings in New Town until a determination could be made as to where a permanent military reservation would be placed.

West Point graduate and former member of the Boundary Survey Commission, Second Lieutenant Thomas Denton Johns arrived in 1849 on the steamer *Panama* with prefabricated structures to build a subsistence depot at La Playa. Johns met with Andrew

B. Gray, former chief surveyor for the American Boundary Survey Commission. Heintzelman then picked out a specific site a few miles south of Old Town for the military buildings near "Punta de los Muertos," and gave Johns the order to move materials and equipment from La Playa.

Late in life, when William Heath Davis told his story of San Diego to a reporter, he said, "I can say that I was its founder." Davis recalled his vision of a beautiful city at the shore of one of the world's great harbors. He indeed brought together a number of individuals in 1850 who provided capital and held similar dreams of a city located south of Old Town. The possibility of turnover of their investments was, however, clearly an incentive.

Prominent local businessmen — Davis, Johns, Gray, José Antonio Aguirre, William C. Ferrell, and Miguel de Pedrorena — bought a section of land they chose to call "New Town."

Top: Two outlying areas drawn for Volume Five of Reports of Explorations and Surveys, *1853-1854, were Santa Isabel (left) and the Valley of San Pasqual (right). Left: Andrew B. Gray was a topographer selected by President Polk for the position of surveyor with the American Boundary Survey Commission. He became one of the founders of New Town. Above: The boundary survey marker at the southwesternmost corner of the United States indicates the international boundary line with Mexico.*

Davis and his partners dedicated a park to the city named Pantoja Park for the man who had drawn the first chart of San Diego Bay in 1782, Don Juan Pantoja y Arriaga of the ship *La Princesa*. Around this park arose the townsite where Davis built his home. The Boston and Pantoja rooming houses, Rosario's Saloon, and seventeen other buildings constructed by civilians and soldiers were intended to give stability to the infant city.

Within the next two years Davis left his business in the hands of others and returned to San Francisco. As the money man, Davis decided his northern enterprises had to be kept going to subsidize the San Diego project. The San Diegans failed him.

Johns left San Diego and resigned from the army. With Davis and Johns out of the picture, the *San Francisco Alta California* reported as early as September 1851 that New Town was a disastrous spectacle.

Between New Town and Old Town lay a strip of land named Middletown encompassing 687 acres along the shoreline of the bay. Ten men paid $3,187 for the property, laid out the streets and city lots, and then waited for boom times to arrive. They made no attempt to build until the Reconstruction period following the American Civil War. Following litigation and the removal of Indians from a "reservation," property began to sell rapidly between 1887 and 1890.

On February 9, 1852, John Russell Bartlett, Boundary Survey commissioner for the United States, entered the harbor landing at La Playa where he took lodging at a small house near the beach.

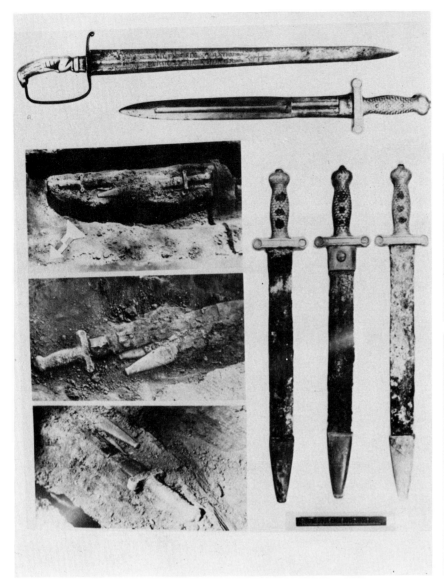

He saw some steamers "merely run in and leave mail, sometimes taking on a supply of coal for the run to San Francisco."

While he was in San Diego, at his request, a band of Diegueño Indians made up of a chief and several of the tribe paid him a visit. There came to Bartlett, a "miserable, ill-looking set, with dark brown complexions and emaciated bodies, and though the weather was cold they were but slightly clad. These people were," he said, "known to the first settlers as the 'Comeya' tribe."

Bartlett described the failure of the town near the shore of the bay which Andrew B. Gray had surveyed, plotted, and shown on the map as "New San Diego." The area consisted of a few substantial frame houses and it served as the depot of the "U.S. Subsistence and the Quarter-Master's Departments." Bartlett puzzled over a large wharf being built at great expense, and wondered what business would bring the vessels there.

He wrote that fresh water did not exist nearer than the San Diego River three miles away. Property owners sank wells but without success. Timber or wood did not exist closer than ten miles, nor could arable land be found within four miles. Bartlett saw that

Above Left: Archaeologists discovered this buried cache of U.S. Army swords while excavating at Mission San Diego. Since the swords date from 1845 to 1865, uncertainty exists as to why they were hidden. In 1861 the federal government allowed Union officers to resign their commissions and join the Confederacy. Were these swords buried by pro-southerners, prior to leaving San Diego, to limit the weaponry of their northern counterparts? Top: A sketch of Old Town in 1856 by Henry Miller. Above: Early adobe construction began with trenches filled with cobblestones and puddled adobe.

Americans Arrive
A New Town Arises

55

Top: Built in 1854, the side-wheeler Orizaba provided service for the Pacific Mail Line. She came into San Diego Harbor in 1858 and for a number of years voyaged between San Diego and San Francisco carrying mail, goat hides, tallow, wool and passengers. She was dismantled in San Francisco in 1887. Above: This 1853 bay view was published in Volume Five of Reports of Explorations and Surveys *to ascertain the most practical and economical route for a railroad from the Mississippi River to the Pacific Ocean.*

"without wood, water, or arable land, the place could never rise to importance."

In 1854 the San Diego and Gila, Southern Pacific and Atlantic Railroad Company was organized with the purpose of utilizing the convenient southern route from San Diego eastward.

Andrew B. Gray had been employed to make an independent southwestern survey for a proposed route in 1853. He still had holdings in New Town. Mayor William H. Emory, brother-in-law of Robert J. Walker, United States senator, and once secretary of the treasury, who backed the route along the thirty-second parallel, owned shares in the "paper town of New San Diego." The Civil War and inadequate financing ended this faintly hopeful project.

The national Panic of 1857 diminished the growth of New Town. The basic cause of failure was over-speculation resulting from the optimism about railroad building. So travelers still had to depend on the slower and much less comfortable ways to get to and from San Diego — by steamship, horseback, or wagon.

In 1857 James Birch began a stage operation between San Antonio, Texas and San Diego, carrying mail and passengers. As the stages reached the Colorado River sand dunes, the passengers switched to riding mules for the trip across the dunes and over the mountains to get to Vallecito Station and Warner's Ranch. San Diegans affectionately called the operation the "Jackass Mail Line." Later the Butterfield stages crossed part of the area and turned northward to San Francisco. (As late as 1915, short line stages ran to Ramona and Lakeside.)

When the American Civil War broke out, what population had remained in New Town dwindled. In 1861, the military depot became a collecting point for soldiers. In early November a mutiny took place among the soldiers at the New San Diego barracks, because of the poor living conditions. Offenders were sent to Alcatraz Island by steamer.

On November 30, 1861, the *Los Angeles Star* reported 400 men encamped at New Town. Troopers from Arizona waited to go by steamer to the east coast, while others who had come from the east coast and San Francisco were scheduled to hold Arizona against the Confederate invasion.

In the winter of 1861–1862, unusually heavy rains — thirty inches — hit the city. The ground around the depot became a quagmire and travel became impossible. Fuel gave out; there appeared no way to replenish the supply. The ultimate humiliation to New Town came as soldiers received orders to tear down the houses and Davis's wharf and warehouse for firewood. By 1866 only five of the original New Town buildings remained.

Alonzo Horton lengthened the wharf, shown here, for access by the Pacific Mail Steamship Company. The first mail ships arrived in September 1872. Shortly after, Horton sold the wharf to the mail company for $45,000.

Americans Arrive
A New Town Arises

57

Top: The U.S. Military Barracks stood at Kettner and Market streets until the late 1920s. Troops utilized the facilities during the Civil, the Spanish-American and First World wars. The several Army units included the supply depot, stables and corrals.
Above: The San Diego Police Department was organized on May 16, 1889. Prior to then, the town was policed by constables. George Pringle, shown here in uniform, was one of about thirty officers on the original force.

Top Left: Dr. David B. Hoffman was the first president of the San Diego County Medical Society, organized in 1870. He was a resident of Old Town. Top Middle: General Samuel P. Heintzelman took part in various Indian skirmishes while stationed in San Diego and Fort Yuma. Top Right: In 1872 Dr. Louis Agassiz accompanied a party of scientists who would be the first to conduct maritime studies on the Pacific. Agassiz became one of San Diego's major boosters. Above Left: William Heath Davis ventured to found New Town near the foot of Market Street shortly after the Mexican War. He left his enterprise in the incapable hands of others and the town collapsed. Above Middle: The mysterious Hannah Horton, circa 1850. Her name appears in neither directories, census returns nor tax rolls, nor was she a relative of Alonzo Horton who would in a quarter of a century begin to develop San Diego. Above Right: Captain Matthew Sherman, arriving in the city as a deputy customs collector, assisted in the formation of the Bank of San Diego, a city park, a school and a residential subdivision.

Americans Arrive
A New Town Arises

Top: In Davis's New Town developers and historians work side by side to update streets and structures and to excavate potentially historical artifacts important to the history of the region. Above: Archaeologists completed excavation of the ruins of the Wetherbee Planing Mill before redevelopment tasks moved in. The historians were able to reconstruct on paper most aspects of the light industrial operation, which was built and destroyed by fire in the late 1880s.

Between May 27 and June 14, 1862, the *Los Angeles Star* reported a remarkable succession of tremors, which reminded San Diego's oldest inhabitants of the quakes that had hit the *presidio* in the year 1812. The shaking earth rocked stores and put cracks in houses, including that of Pio Pico and the Whaley House. At the mouth of the bay, a wave rushed three feet beyond the line of the tide. Even the tower of the lighthouse on Point Loma was severely cracked. The river at Old Town overflowed its banks a few feet.

On May 27 alone, seven quakes hit the town and turned the scene into one of terror. People rushed from their houses to the streets and to the Old Town plaza, many remaining at prayer.

During the American Civil War, San Diego was virtually shut off from the rest of the world. There was no newspaper and stage lines had been shut down; only an occasional ship or a new troop of soldiers brought news of events. However, by 1867 developers began to show an interest in the town again. Some still expressed hopes that it would be the terminus of a transcontinental railroad.

Equally as important as excavation of the Wetherbee Planing Mill (left) the view on the right portrays the unearthing of an outhouse by a member of the San Diego Science Foundation in 1981. Incredibly, these facilities provide a unique source of cultural familiarity. This one was located in Block 44 of New Town, circa 1850. The trenching machine, a backhoe with a twenty-four-inch bucket, digs alongside the areas determined for excavation. In this instance, the pit reached a depth of twenty feet.

Americans Arrive
A New Town Arises

The cornerstone of the original San Diego Courthouse was laid August 12, 1871. The superb structure had forty-two stained-glass windows depicting the seals of the states admitted to the Union at that time. While the building is no longer extant, the windows have been preserved. Topping the cupola was the figure of Justice with blindfold and holding scales. Below him the figures of presidents Washington, Lincoln, Grant and Garfield presided over the four corners of the main roof. In 1942 a local resident bought the statues and situated them in front of three houses he had built in Middletown. One by one they were stolen, although one statue has been relocated. The courthouse building was demolished in 1959.

CHAPTER 4

Horton's Addition Opens the Land

IN APRIL 15, 1867, the bearded, thick-set Alonzo Erastus Horton arrived in San Diego, a place the Connecticut Yankee called "Heaven-on-Earth." Horton came prepared to bring the moribund board of trustees to life. He put his money down and bought 960 acres of what is now downtown San Diego for 27.5¢ an acre. He advertised widely, gave lots to people who could develop their holdings, offered free quarter lots to those who promised to build houses, and donated land to churches.

Horton saw the harbor as a great natural asset and thought wharves to be of immense aid in the development of the new town site. His wharf at the foot of Fifth Street came to be the entrance to the city in the nineteenth century.

Real estate madness hit San Diego. The 226 blocks of Horton's Addition sold with such rapidity that he complained of handling so much money. Some buyers lived in tents until they could clear off their property. Speculation ran rampant as property turned over, sometimes sight unseen. There was no "buyer's remorse" at this time.

On February 16, 1868, city officials meeting to determine how to provide park lands for the city at first thought to set aside in perpetuity 160 acres of mesa land but instead reserved 1,400 acres close to the city. A common practice in the great cities of the

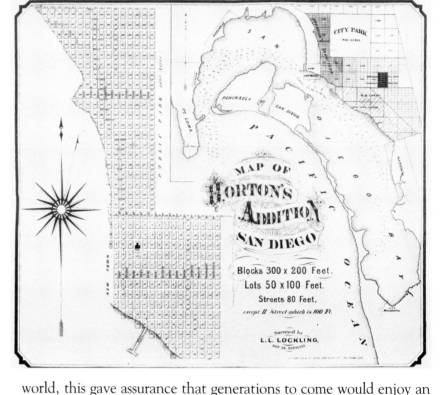

Top: A sketch of San Diego looking southwest from the mesa toward the bay, about 1872. Above left: The far-seeing Alonzo Horton brought about the first major, planned development of San Diego. Above Right: Although a few oversights in planning were to plague Horton's Addition, the 226-block development transformed San Diego into a boom town.

San Diego
An Illustrated History

world, this gave assurance that generations to come would enjoy an unruffled green belt in the heart of their city. The State Legislature confirmed their action, resulting in the formal creation of "Balboa Park," in 1911.

To step up his plans for development of the city, Horton built a hotel between Third and Fourth streets on Broadway in 1870. The focus of the city to that time had been along Fifth Street to the south between Broadway and the harbor. Horton, however, intended that Broadway to the west become the main artery of the city.

When *The San Diego Union* issued its first edition on October 10, 1868, the editors, William Gatewood and Edward Bushyhead,

advertised the climate, an emphasis not totally coincidental. Horton knew well the need of a fulcrum to boost his town.

Dr. Henry Griffin, writing in the *Pacific Medical Journal* said:

The inhabitants have secured a large stock of thermometers and pluviometers and have zealous meteorologists, and [are] determined to demonstrate the unparalleled sanitary values of their growing burgh. Thus far San Diego has led the race and presents the strongest inducements to valetudinarians.

Midwesterners might not have understood the language, but they could relate a hope for better health to the climate of San Diego. And for many, health meant life in the back country.

While pride, enthusiasm, and promoters sparked the inner-city growth, other forces pushed the outlying areas. A gold strike at Julian in 1869 – 1870 brought new prospectors and residents. For ten years Julian stood as a center of gold mining, but that activity waned.

The San Diego Irrigation Company formed to provide water for the lands of the Valley of El Cajon, and the San Diego Flume Company brought liquid gold to the city. In El Cajon Valley, where Isaac Lankershim had subdivided an old land grant, ranchers rented space to boarders with ailments, and taught those who had lost hope of recovering their health to farm citrus, avocados, and grapes. In the next decade, asthmatics, rheumatics, and those suffering respiratory ailments would find the back country a sanctuary. For them, light agricultural work became a source of income and a way to regain their pride.

Matthew Sherman, New Town resident, had served as a soldier since before 1851. In 1867 he bought 320 acres from the city and subdivided it. The area was known then as Sherman's Addition, later as East San Diego, and still later as Golden Hills. By May 1868, the Shermans had moved into their home at the rim of

Originally from New York, Alonzo Erastus Horton made his first trip to California in 1851 and allowed sixteen years to pass before he returned to make history in San Diego. His early investments styled the configuration of downtown. Wharves blossomed on the harbor to accommodate heavy trade and the population came in droves to buy up the properties in Horton's Addition.

Horton's Addition

Top: Passengers hustle for the streetcar at the foot of Fifth Street, circa 1886. Above Left: Moving between political and business careers, William S. Rosecrans promoted the southern California railroads. Both a fort and a main thoroughfare bear his name today. Above Right: Although these men surveyed for the San Diego and Yuma line in 1872, setbacks postponed the completion of the railroad for another ten years.

the brush-covered hillside east of downtown. It became a neighborhood of richly designed homes.

In June 1869, Frank, Levi, and Warren Kimball negotiated to acquire Rancho de la Nación, twenty-seven thousand acres near the south end of San Diego Bay. They subdivided, laid out a town, and by 1871 had built a wharf. Within ten years vessels such as the *Trafalgar* and the *Rover* from Antwerp had berthed there.

Another force served to consolidate the growing prosperity of San Diego when in 1867 the citizens heard that the Memphis and El Paso (the route controlled by General John C. Frèmont) would link San Diego's shipping with the long sought Southern Pacific Railway.

In the last week of September 1869, Mr. William H. Seward, former governor of New York, U.S. senator, and secretary of state

These streetcar passengers rounded the corner of Fifth and Market streets in 1887, when the first electric streetcar line went into operation.

to Presidents Lincoln and Johnson arrived by steamer at San Diego. In the greeting party were General William Starke Rosecrans, then U.S. minister to Mexico; General Thomas S. Sedgwick; and General M.C. Hunter, and others connected with the Southern Pacific Railroad. Carriages took the Sewards to the residence of Mr. McDonald of south San Diego, along with the generals, Representatives Samuel Beach Axtell from California, and Logan Holt Roots from Arkansas. Mr. Henry Fitch and others went to the Franklin House at Old Town to await them.

In the afternoon Mr. Carr and Mr. Bush called upon Seward, whereupon the governor proposed to go to Old Town, saying that he was eager to see the oldest city in California. From there they went to see the "Old Mission." Seward told Judge Thomas Henry Bush he would prefer to "lose his dinner" rather than miss seeing the spot so sacred in all the first associations with civilization in California.

Seward and those who met with him selected a site for a proposed station near the Horton wharf. Later the plan for the railroad aborted as more powerful interests, whose political plans did not include the port village of San Diego, acquired the rights to the railroad. While this left San Diego still without a solid overland transportation system, vessels at least continued to use the undeveloped harbor.

By an Act of Congress on March 3, 1847, steamers of the subsidized Pacific Mail Steamship Company had to make San

Above: Australian schooners carrying coal to San Diego in the 1880s were soon to be replaced by oil-bearing steamers. Right: This lithograph by A.L. Bancroft and Company entitled "Bird's Eye View of San Diego" appeared in 1876. Although the vaquero at bottom right is somewhat fanciful, the balance of the illustration is useful, and accurately portrays the Spanish Bight, a watered area between Coronado and North Island which existed until World War II. Gradually, land filled the region but for a time a wooden railroad trestle and bridge spanned the two islands.

San Diego
An Illustrated History

Diego one of the stops to pick up mail. The first steamer to enter the harbor was the P.M.S.C. *Oregon* on March 30, 1849. By 1869, when Horton had become involved in San Diego, the construction boom caused schooners to bring a great deal of lumber out of the Pacific Northwest.

With the boom, ships came carrying coal from Newcastle, New South Wales, and Wellington, New Zealand. Vessels brought cement and steel and patent fertilizer from England and Germany and glass from Belgium. By the mid-1880s coal was on the way out and oil in.

J. Ross Browne, a world-traveling journalist, wrote in *The San Diego Union* in August 1871:

I am so thoroughly persuaded that property in the vicinity of San Diego will be of enormous value within three years from this date that I have determined to retain a large interest in my track of town lots, for I believe there is a fortune in them. . . . San Diego is now . . . the most attractive point for investment and speculation on the Pacific Coast, or, so far as I know, in the United States.

Jean Louis Rudolph Agassiz, the eminent nineteenth-century Swiss-American naturalist wrote of the emerging town in August 1872. While in San Diego with a party of scientists from the East who were exploring and searching for specimens of animal life he observed:

There is one advantage that I, as a scientific man may lay more stress upon than is necessary; but I hardly think it possible. It is the question of latitude. You are here upon the thirty-second parallel, beyond the reach of the severe winters of the higher latitudes. This is your capital, and it is worth millions to you.

For all the praise about the qualities of San Diego, in but a brief five years after Horton's arrival, Old Town declined rapidly. It had

Above: The artist of this 1873 lithograph captured a deceptive but common view of the city when late afternoon shadows seem to draw the mountains much closer to the coast. The view is from Point Loma looking eastward. Right: William Jorres was born in Hanover, Germany, in 1824. He reached San Diego by way of Buenos Aires and San Francisco, and joined in the construction boom of the 1860s. He and a partner, S.S. Culverwell, built the wharf at the foot of F Street and Jorres conducted business associated with the wharf. He also served as county treasurer for seven years.

Above Left: Dr. P. C. Remondino served as city physician in 1875-1876 and active surgeon for the California-Southern Railroad Company and the Pacific Coast Steamship Company. One of his contributions to San Diego was the founding of a major hospital in 1879. Regretfully, competition with charitable institutions injured business and the hospital was abandoned. Above Right: In 1888 firemen parked the all-new La France Steam Pumper before Fire Station Number One, between Third Street and Broadway.

Above Left and Left: City Hall took over the offices formerly occupied by Consolidated National Bank in the late 1890s. The bank building, originally a two-story brick structure completed in 1874, was built by William Jorres for $16,635. In 1882 the San Diego Public Library moved into the second floor with about 7,000 volumes. Major remodeling and the addition of two more stories transpired shortly before the bank and the library moved out. City Hall kept its offices at the Fifth and G streets location until 1938. Historians believe it may be the oldest structure extant in the Gaslamp District. Above: Horses pulled heavy sprinkler barrels down Fifth Street, circa 1890.

Horton's Addition

In the late 1800s growers planted
more than half a million fruit
trees in the outlying valleys and
sold their produce in the city's agricultural district. The availability
of affordable land made agriculturalists of many immigrants. By
the 1940s, Japanese immigrants
to San Diego had become an important part of commercial agriculture.

had virtually no chance of becoming the center of a revitalized
city, sitting at the edge of the mud flats too far from the bay. To
the west the San Diego River blocked growth as did a ridge to
the north and east.

Then, as if to make sure that it would not rise again, a final
blow was struck the old *pueblo*. *The San Diego Union* of April 21,
1872, reported that a fire of disastrous proportions had started in
the Old Town courthouse and roared through the Colorado House,
the Franklin House (the first three-story hotel west of the Mississippi), Schiller's, Asher's, and Dan Clark's Saloon. A hook-and-
ladder company arrived, but the water pumps on the plaza failed.
For some time the business people who had lost their stores sold
goods out of stalls in the plaza.

William Henry Bishop, a writer for *New Monthly Harpers
Magazine*, who arrived in San Diego aboard a steamer one year

after the Old Town fire, described the condition of Old Town: "The earth-works of Commodore Stockton, who threw them up one night before the enemy knew he was here, could still be seen on the hill."

Bishop saw the still toppled flagstaff in the plaza in Old Town and the decayed music stand and across the street the shambles of burned out buildings which no one thought important enough to rebuild. He saw the shutters nailed up and thought the town desolate.

"The broken Merchant's Exchange will never supply cocktails to thirsty souls again," he said; "the Cosmopolitan Hotel, though wrecked only financially is without a guest; whole rows of weather-beaten adobe houses — whole quarters of them stand vacant. It should be a famous place for ghosts."

Bishop wrote impartially; he also had negative views of Horton's Addition and thought the Horton House to be disproportionately large, built in anticipation of future greatness which proved to be a loss to its proprietors. The blue shades had come down, and the plate glass windows were dusty in much of the Horton Block opposite, but they still wore an expectant look, and "guests had a charming view of the harbor and the deep blue ocean."

The location of Horton's wharf at the foot of Fifth Street inspired construction to rise along that street northward, and Horton himself added a dozen major buildings to the scene.

Above Left: Robert O'Neill and his family gathered on the second-story porch of the American Hotel in Old Town for this 1886 portrayal. A few of the tenants, including "Bum," the town mascot who loved booze as much as an old bone, lazed in the sun's rays. This photograph recently assisted historians in identifying the locations of the pump and well, discovered by site archaeologists. It will also allow for an accurate restoration of the building. Above Right: The view north on Fifth Street from K Street is virtually a ghost town in this 1875 photograph. Wide streets, wooden sidewalks and protruding porches curiously lack activity.

Horton's Addition

73

Top: The Old Mission Olive Factory was built in 1915 by R. S. Truffley to fit in with the concept of Old Town and the Panama-California Exposition structures. This structure was later razed and replaced by the Cal-Trans Building. Above Left: As one of the many easterners who migrated to the California gold fields in the 1840s, Ephraim W. Morse discovered prospecting to be back-breaking work. He soon traveled south and became an associate judge of the Court of Sessions of San Diego and a practicing lawyer in the Court of the Judicial District. He represented San Diego in its disputed survey of the Pueblo lands. In business, he helped to found the Consolidated National Bank and the Bank of San Diego.

Above Right: Prior to his terms as county assessor, state senator and sheriff of San Diego County, James McCoy headed a team to survey the Colorado desert. He arrived in the U.S. from Ireland in 1842.

San Diego
An Illustrated History

The passions Americans have for surveying, staking out, fencing, and recording property kept all sorts of tradesmen busy. Corner lots, rectangular blocks, and other peculiarities dear to property owners of that time took shape. Two things haunted latter-day urban planners, however — the lack of alleys and the very small city blocks of the Horton Addition. Neither did the thought of small inner-city parks occur, except for the two or three in downtown.

The common council dealt with various issues as the need for regulations arose concerning street paving, utilities, horse-and-cart traffic, health matters, fire and building codes, and the moving of buildings from one site to another.

Top: Three-thousand people jammed the entrance to the Los Baños Plunge on opening day in 1897. The intriguing Moorish structure, which once stood at Broadway and Kettner Street, housed Russian and Turkish baths. Above: The home of María Reyes Ybañez was built in 1821 at the corner of Juan and Washington streets in Old Town.

Horton's Addition

Following a 1902 survey expedition in the Gulf of California, the crew of the U.S.S. Ranger gathered in San Diego shortly before the cruiser was decommissioned.

No question that Horton's Addition had fostered within local government the change from a small town, do-it-yourself approach which functioned without such details as building permits or plans, to an awareness of the need to centralize and control a city on the verge of a growth explosion.

This boom quieted down in 1873 with the news that the proposed Texas and Pacific Railroad organized by Colonel Thomas A. Scott had been lost to San Diego. Scott had come to the city on August 20, 1872, full of enthusiasm and brought with him an impressive party which included governors and senators. The "Railroad King" led the party to the Horton House while reporters covering the event from San Francisco hovered around. Black Friday and the Panic of 1873 dashed any hopes of a railroad terminus at San Diego.

SAM BIBO AND ONE DAY'S CATCH OF SEA BASS AT HOTEL DEL CORONADO DEC. 4, 1905.

REDUCTION IN RATES!

THE PACIFIC MAIL STEAMSHIP CO'S

FAVORITE SIDE-WHEEL STEAMSHIP

SENATOR

Fare to Santa Barbara, San Pedro and San Diego,

CABIN $5. **STEERAGE, $3.**

CHAS. THORN, Commander.

Will leave the Company's Wharf, corner First and Brannan streets, on

THURSDAY, Oct. 1st, 1874, at 9 o'clock, A. M.

FOR

SAN DIEGO!

CALLING AT

San Simeon, San Luis Obispo, Santa Barbara, San Buenaventura, San Pedro (Los Angeles), and Anaheim.

NO EXTRA CHARGE FOR MEALS OR STATEROOMS.

FREIGHT, To Santa Barbara, San Pedro, Anaheim and San Diego, $2.00 PER TON.

STEAMER "CALIFORNIA,"

CAPTAIN STOTHARD,

For Freight Combustibles and Stock only, will sail from Wharf, corner of First and Brannan Streets, on WEDNESDAY, September 30th, at 5 P. M., for San Pedro and Anaheim, calling at San Luis Obispo, Santa Barbara and San Buenaventura.

FREIGHT TO SANTA BARBARA, SAN PEDRO & ANAHEIM, $1.50 PER TON

Combustibles and Coal Oil at Special Rates.

Company's Office, Cor. Sacramento & Leidesdorff Sts.

That panic had begun in Europe with the collapse of banks in Vienna. In this country the railroad companies built recklessly. Iron companies followed suit and overexpanded. Western farmers bought heavily on credit, and the panic reached America on September 18, when the bank house of Jay Cooke and Company folded in New York. The depression which followed lasted five years. By the end of the year 1874, railroad construction completely halted and unemployment rose. For two more years the failure rate of businesses remained high.

For about five years the city languished; some maintained that Horton was broke and San Diego bankrupt. Following every decline, however, San Diego managed to slow down the public improvements which fostered growth; the full impact of depressions never struck.

Carlsbad, only thirty miles north of San Diego, was settled in this decade, and the railroad company built a station and shipped water from the newly organized Carlsbad Land and Mineral Water Company to other parts of the county. A station was founded at Leucadia in 1875, named for a small island off the coast of Greece: Leucatia, the Isle of Paradise.

In 1879, Frank Kimball of National City went to Boston to encourage the president of the Santa Fe Railroad to bring the subsidiary California-Southern Railroad to San Diego. Kimball represented a group of local investors who guaranteed three million dol-

Above Left: For a time, guests of the Hotel del Coronado and local residents could take hotel-sponsored fishing trips off the Coronado Islands. Often the day's catch would be put on the blocks and any number of individuals would line up to have their pictures taken by the hotel photographer. Above Right: On March 3, 1847, an Act of Congress ruled that San Diego become a regular mail stop for steamers of the Pacific Mail Steamship Company. Two years later the first steamer, the P.M.S.C. Oregon, entered the harbor.

The U.S. Post Office building at 320 West F Street was designed by James Knox Taylor of Knoxville, Tennessee. Taylor was previously senior draftsman in the office of the supervising architect for the U.S. Treasury Department. He selected an adaptation of Spanish Colonial architecture reflecting the history, climate and traditions of the state. Opening ceremonies were held on April 5, 1913, and Dorothy Bartholomew, daughter of the postmaster, hoisted the stars and stripes on the east tower of the building. The young woman had a difficult time holding her balance on the narrow ledge, but she managed to jerk the halyards with sufficient force to break the ensign.

lars in cash and seven million dollars in land to bring the line to San Diego. The arrival of this transcontinental line on November 21, 1885 opened the Boom of the Eighties.

The city's port facilities bulged with imported lumber, bridge timbers, coal, cement, and other products to be distributed throughout Southern California.

At last the railroad made it possible for those nineteenth-century travelers who came to California in comparative comfort to arrive at a place where they could miraculously recover their health or find a fortune in land — realizing the visions of the Spaniards three hundred years earlier.

Telephone lines, rimming these hillside lots, accompanied San Diego into the twentieth century. In 1904 the expansive harbor received international carriers and a transcontinental railroad delivered opportunists and health seekers to the far-west utopia.

Horton's Addition

In 1887 Fifth Street was the main thoroughfare of the city. Horse-drawn streetcars and buckboards meandered in the bustle of shipping, commerce and wholesale activities taking place at the Steamship wharf. The Pacific Coast Steamship Company wharf was constructed in 1878, and four years later work had begun on the "T." This site connected with Horton's Wharf by a railroad with undersized rails and low horse-drawn flatcars. Nearby a warehouse stored surplus freight. The steamship company continued to do business in the same location until 1956.

CHAPTER 5

The Boom and the Bust

INLAND OVER THE RISE from the beach where the climate is drier and temperature ten degrees higher than along the shoreline, the village of Poway, location of the famous *Painted Rocks*, was started in the 1880s by a wave of new immigrants. In places like this and Guatay Valley, invalids regained their physical and mental health by working their own land and growing citrus trees or varieties of fruits which required sheltered nooks, lots of sunshine, and the sweet labor of aching bodies. Turned into agriculturalists, they became the new advocates for immigration into Southern California.

The ailing took up homesteads at Alpine and in the El Cajon Valley where they had gone, as one pioneer put it, to "Expiration Hills." Land came cheap, and the water, while marginal, meant at least irrigation. In this way regions opened up that otherwise would probably not have been tilled for several decades more.

Del Mar blossomed in 1882. The first settlers came to Imperial Beach in the eighties when George Chaffee, the self-educated engineering genius, bought a large section of the area to develop as a summer retreat. Chaffee, the founder of Etiwanda and Ontario, is better known as the developer of irrigation in the Colorado River area. Oceanside began during the booms of the 1880s

San Diego
An Illustrated History

as a coastal resort town and developed in the 1920s as a small business and residential region.

Lakeside was mapped out by planners in 1886 on a forty-five-acre parcel of land. In 1886, the Lakeside Inn, a resort hotel, was built by the El Cajon Valley Land Company, since the region had been planned to establish health resort activities. A rail line, the San Diego, Cuyamaca and Eastern Railroad, in time became a part of the San Diego and Arizona Eastern Railway which operated trains through Lakeside to Foster, about three miles distant.

The founding of Pacific Beach at the south end of Mission Bay took place in the summer of 1887, with advertisements describing 2,500 lots being sold in three days, even before the property had been surveyed. By October 1887, prices for the property had climbed. The featured attraction, the Cliff Hotel, was completed in that year. Advertisements promised a motor line from Old Town and "other extras."

Ocean Beach had a rush on land sales at about the same time, and *The San Diego Union* reported that "the locality of Eden was lost to the world until Carlson and Higgins discovered Ocean Beach."

The Land and Town Company created Escondido to help sell that north county area, and La Mesa began when the San Diego Flume Company bought four thousand acres in 1887 to raise money

Top: As soon as the Fifth Street entrance to San Diego had begun to develop, Alonzo Horton built the Horton House on Broadway (D Street). This photograph was taken in 1880.

Middle: An 1880 illustration depicts the yet undeveloped Horton Plaza fronting Horton House. It is alleged that Helen Hunt Fiske Jackson penned Ramona while staying in the hotel.

Above: For a period, Mission San Diego fell prey to local settlers who pilfered timber and brick. Used by the Army between 1850 and 1865, the mission is an active parish today.

The Boom and the Bust

Top Left: Colonel Jacob Shell Taylor arrived in San Diego in November 1882 and six months later purchased the Los Penasquitos Ranch. Shortly afterward, 130 Durham cattle and 10 Thoroughbred horses arrived to comprise the nucleus of his stock. In 1885 he became owner of the Del Mar townsite, importing lumber to build cottages and sinking wells. Above Left: Frank T. Botsford, the father of La Jolla. Above Right: From Third Street the view extends to Point Loma and North Island, still barren in the 1800s. The U.S. Military Barracks perched on the bay on State Street, with Wetherbee's Planing Mill to the right. The gas arc lamp in the foreground was an interesting, though a short-lived, experiment.

from subdivision sales. The momentum for the westward immigration came through the railroad promotion — colorful posters, calendars, and booster literature distributed in the East and Midwest.

Encinitas, located on the coast 14 miles south of Oceanside, was heavily advertised during the summer of 1887. Sorrento Valley, better known as a light industrial sector, is considered coastal despite its location 2.5 miles inland. Placed on the plateau south of the Torrey Pines grade, it had a start just off the then new route of the California Southern Railroad. The local paper reported that Sorrento Valley had land that would grow anything in the world with or without irrigation. But those who worked with country problems did not yet have to be concerned with the major tasks of city fathers.

The developing inner city brought gas and telegraph service to its citizens in 1881–1882; the first transcontinental train arrived from the East on November 21, 1885; the first horse-drawn streetcar pulled on a two-mile line along Fifth Street on July 4, 1886; and the electric lights came on in that same year. The first electric streetcar line went into operation in 1887 and the first modern dam in 1888.

In 1886 more than three hundred buildings were completed in Horton's Addition. In October 1886 alone, real estate transactions totaled a record high of over $1,000,000, or an average of $18,488

Above: Pioneer real estate salesmen Robert J. Pennell (shown here) and Frank T. Botsford erected a tent and took turns posing with a spyglass on the land they would develop as La Jolla Park. Apparently, the two camped out in the tent, which held cans of corned beef, vegetables and a jug containing liquid refreshment.

Left: This downtown view, taken in 1885, extends from Sixth and Market Streets toward the future location of the Coronado Bay Bridge.

The Boom and the Bust

Top: Although the horse-drawn bus was advertised as San Diego and Coronado Transfer Company Rail, it moved passengers and sightseers all over the coastal towns. Gaily painted, much like the stagecoaches of this and earlier times, the photo depicts the bus awaiting passengers at the Ocean Beach Hotel. Above: Two sources originate for the name of the border Mexican city. Indians referred to the area as teguana, meaning a place of no food, and Spaniards pronounced it Tijuana. A second source suggests that the name is derived from two Spanish words, Tia and Jane, literally "Aunt Jane." The lady was famous for her meals, inspiring the locals to immortalize her. The photo shows the American side of Tia Juana in 1887.

per day. In a single week lots rose from $200 to $1,000. Although for a time material shortages slowed down construction, the sounds of hammers, rasps of saws, and the mason's trowel cut the air.

The Santa Fe depot was built in 1887, and by 1888 the region had street improvements, churches, schools, and new homes completed in Golden Hills, Middletown, and Coronado. Victorian gingerbreads lined many streets. Some had widow's walks, solar heating (later replaced by electricity), and domed spires; most had hardwood floors, stained glass; and each one proclaimed its owner's wealth and social standing.

The city boomed and as railroad fares were reduced, speculators helped immigrants to get to the city. In the mid-eighties the population jumped from five thousand to thirty-five thousand. But not only the rails transported people and goods.

Top: The short-lived Royal Hotel was located at Eighth and National avenues. Above: The ferry steamer Coronado *left San Francisco and arrived in San Diego in August 1886, the same year the Coronado Ferry Company was incorporated. She was 104 feet long with an 85 horse-power engine of 5 foot stroke. She ran every half hour.*

The Boom and the Bust

A German gym class in 1898. Verein Entract was organized in 1885 and reorganized as San Diego Turnverein in 1886. On June 23, 1889 Phoenix Turnverein was organized, and on February 12, 1890 Concordia Turnverein combined its membership with the Phoenix group. J. H. Fred Heilbron became the first president of these organizations. About 1910 Germania Hall was built in San Diego; its officers and members served the public schools by teaching physical culture, training techniques, and physical development skills to thousands of young people.

The Episcopal Bishop of San Francisco, William I. Kip, described the San Diego-bound steamers filled with "hopeful consumptives, local realty promoters, and financiers who had connected health and community progress."

Author, lawyer, and former Minnesota assemblyman Theodore Strong Van Dyke, who came with the health seekers, wrote in a booklet in 1887:

. . . land where such a change in values can be so sudden and so great is certainly beyond any ordinary standard of value. It erects its own standard and compels all old-time political economy and business principles to bow to it. There is but one Southern California on earth; a residence there is a luxury, the amount of land is limited; people will have it, therefore, it commands the price of a luxury.

Coronado became the outstanding boom project in the San Diego area. The peninsula which protects San Diego harbor from the ocean is a strip of land culminating at the northern end in a large sandy space. This brush-covered site had not been used until 1885, when Elisha S. Babcock, who had heard of the place as a health seeker's paradise, transformed the peninsula into a new city. Babcock arrived in 1884, looked over the region, and decided to build a million-dollar hotel. He obtained capital from Illinois, organized a syndicate, purchased seven thousand acres of land for $110,000, and embarked on an extensive advertising campaign.

Above: Seven unidentified men lined up in front of a liquor store in 1887 making an interesting character study of the times. While nearly all sported beards, and all but one wore proper coat and hat, the viewer can only guess at their particular professions. Left: These lemon pickers were typical of the health boom settlers who came to the dry mild climate of the back country between 1880 and 1900.

The Boom and the Bust

A local photographic gallery carried a variety of costumes for individuals who wanted their photos taken in a western mode. Here four ladies posed in bloomers suits for a stock photograph, as they pretended to smoke, drink and play cards. Notice the ace protruding from one lady's calfskin legging.

Above: Ah Quin, shown here with his family in 1899, came to San Diego about 1879. When track for the railroad was being laid from National City to San Bernardino, Ah Quin served as foreman, and later he opened a restaurant in town. In time he became honorary mayor of San Diego's Chinatown. Left: Babcock and Spreckels built the Morena Dam, delivering to the city a ten years' supply of water at four cents per thousand gallons.

Above: Elisha Spurr Babcock, Jr., and his two sons. Originally from Indiana, Babcock was president of the San Diego Water Company, president of the Western Salt Works, president of the Coronado Beach Company and the Coronado Gas and Electric Works. He was vice president of the Coronado Railroad Company and the Coronado Ferry Company. He is remembered today as the principal owner and builder of the legendary Hotel del Coronado. Opposite: History is indebted to these portrait subjects *who, although unidentified, left their impressions for future generations to study. Both portraits were taken in 1895.*

Chicago Art Gallery,
Klindt & Walters.

657 Fifth Street, Bet. G & H,
SAN DIEGO, CAL.

In 1888 the Hotel del Coronado added beauty to a barren mesquite-covered "island" inhabited by gophers and jackrabbits. Babcock and Hampton L. Story promoted land sales through their Coronado Beach Company, set up real estate tents, and had a field day as balloons soared over the bay. They used every design known to land sellers as they sold over one million-dollars worth of Coronado lots.

John D. and Adolph Spreckels came to San Diego for a vacation in 1887. The sons of Claus Spreckels of San Francisco ("Sugar King" of Hawaii) were impressed with the city, and they had millions to invest in the local economy. But the significance of the

Above: Perched atop forty acres of orchards and lawns, the ornate three-story Paradise Valley Sanatarium opened about 1887 as a popular resort. At that time the investment in buildings and land was reputed to be more than $150,000. In 1904, Seventh Day Adventists took over operation of the sanatarium which accommodated sixty-five patients or guests, forty nurses and six doctors. Right: The young and enchanting Kate Sessions, circa 1871, is known as the mother of Balboa Park. By the late 1880s she had established a botanical garden in Coronado and a nursery in the Hillcrest area from which she contributed to the landscape of Balboa Park, Horton Plaza and Maple Canyon.

Spreckels's influence lay in their enthusiasm, optimism, and the example the brothers set as they went to work and established the Spreckels Brothers Commercial Company. In time their interests controlled water developments, some twenty-five streetcar lines, and the newspaper.

But pride turned to fear in the winter of 1887. The following spring building slowed down, and as in the rest of California, construction business sluffed off in San Diego. The San Diego *Golden Era* supplement of 1888 praised what had been accomplished and deftly sidestepped any mention of a suggested economic collapse.

Certainly special issues of the *San Diego Sun* and *San Diego Bee* listed improvements from business blocks to mining activities and praised the growers who had planted over half a million fruit

Top Left: As head of the San Diego Land and Town Company, William Dickinson (left) founded Chula Vista. He is shown here with F. A. Kimball. Top Right: A top-knotted hairstyle, stand-up collar and epaulettes date this unidentified woman's portrait to about 1895. Above: The spacious back country of Poway attracted many away from San Diego.

The Boom and the Bust

95

Ulysses S. Grant, Jr., the oldest son of the President, migrated west with his wife in 1892 and bought a home, pictured here, at Seventh and Ash streets. The three-story mansion was formerly owned by Ora Hubbell, a local banker. In time Grant bought the Horton House and built the still prestigious U.S. Grant Hotel. His home at Seventh and Ash is the site of the present-day El Cortez Hotel.

trees in the back country. *The San Diego Union* tracked building permits and construction daily, and throughout the year 1889 considerable activity took place except during periods of bad weather. The paper did hint late in the year that there had been a reduction in building in the "wake of abnormal construction activity of 1887 – 1888."

In 1890 the building and real estate sales hit their lowest ebb. Assessments dropped from forty million dollars to twenty-five million in two years. The economy had become uneven and while some industries had held up, others were in difficulty. U.S. companies fell short on capital. Prices of steel and iron products declined and employment levels dropped.

In 1891 the California National Bank went under and the next year other local banks were hit hard. In 1893 the National Bank Panic hit the city. Some one hundred railroad corporations failed as did six hundred banks, and Coxey's army marched on Washington, D.C.

Top: The Carpenter Gothic Sherman-Gilbert House was originally located at 138 Fir Street, and later moved to Heritage Park, an area set aside by the county for placement of his-torical buildings. John Sherman, builder, and John B. Stannard, architect, wove intricate detail into their 1889 design including a full-circle parlor window topped by a frieze of stained glass. Mr. and Mrs. A. H. Gilbert bought the home in 1897.
Above: When the boom of the 1880s fell short, every real estate company in the directory had a listing on this property at Fourth and Elm streets.

Above: San Diego about 1890, looking northward on Fifth Street. Electricity and gas lamps had already illuminated certain parts of town. Horse-drawn buggies ambled lazily alongside streetcars which carried passengers to the outlying mesas and rapidly developing residential districts. Right: The Gothic James S. Gordon residence at 2505 D Avenue in National City, about 1889. Among other of Gordon's business and political endeavors, he worked with the chamber of commerce and San Francisco businessmen to arrange for steamers to stop at the National City wharf.

San Diego
An Illustrated History

98

Top: This residence, referred to as the Grey Stone Castle, was located at Fifth and Juniper streets and was built for D. D. Dare, who had organized the California National Bank in 1888. When the bank failed a few years later, to no one's sur- prise Dare fled to Europe. The receiver for the bank had the re- sponsibility of disposing of the castle and sold it to John H. Gay, owner of the Lakeside Hotel. Above: Governor Robert Waterman and other officials rode in small flat boats, protect- ing themselves with parasols, in an opening-day celebration of the San Diego Flume. The 36-mile redwood structure, completed in 1888, cost more than $1.3 mil- lion and ran from a diversion dam to Eucalyptus Reservoir in the Grossmont area.

The Grand Hotel, completed in 1888, is significant for its architectural style as well as its historical association with the boom of 1887. It is one of two examples remaining in San Diego of the Baroque Revival or Second Empire style. It was recorded by the Historical American Building Survey in 1975 and is designated San Diego Historical Site Number Ninety-five.

Significant civic improvements had been made, however, which would last into the next century. The city itself had grown to the status of a small, modern community, and in the surrounding county regions, more than eighty towns and villages stood as symbols of potential growth ready to burst into twentieth-century greatness. Temporarily the impetus slowed as the nation became embraced in a "nuisance war."

The war between Spain and the United States began on April 23, 1898, and the patriotism of San Diegans shone brightly as volunteer companies were organized at Chula Vista, Coronado, National City, San Diego, and other local communities.

"Colonel" U.S. Grant Jr., became the key man who led the San Diego "Minute Men" off to war. Just five years earlier he had brought his family to the city for his wife's health. A successful real estate promoter and a wealthy taxpayer, he would build the U.S. Grant Hotel on the site of the old Horton House as a memorial to his father.

Top: A tattered advertising display adjoins the offices of the San Diego Gas and Electric Company in this 1890 photo. Above: Logs, shipped by sea and then cut and planed, were hauled onto hitched wagons and transported over rough roads to the back communities of Julian and Ramona. Left: Parrott & Erb advertised modern transportation in this 1896 brochure.

The Boom and the Bust

The Pacific Coast Steamship Company (top) and the Santa Fe Steamship Company wharves snaked more than one thousand feet over the water, carrying flatcars to expedite freight shipment. Until the first transcontinental railroad reached San Diego in 1884, the city's fine natural harbor provided the major avenue for commercial expansion. The harbor is still a thriving commercial success today.

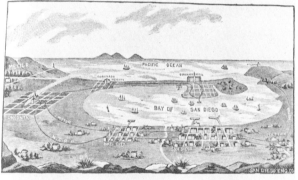

ONEONTA!

BY THE SEA!

From April until August 1898, the papers carried news of the Minute Men's daily activities at Camp Merritt in Northern California. Locally, fortifications were improved at Ballast Point where a company of the Seventh Regiment was stationed.

As if to signal the end of the century, when John Minter returned from the war in Cuba, he found that his wife Serafina and mother-in-law Juana Machado de Wrightington had given up their old adobe home in Old Town to move to Coronado with relatives. The Spanish period structure lay in crumbled ruins. Juana, who had seen the Americans arrive during the Mexican War, had taken in the wounded of General Kearny's army for recuperation, and had cared for Captain Hunter's son to manhood, was the last of her generation. She closed the book on Old Town.

Left: The original Point Loma Lighthouse, built in November 1855. Top Right: The gold fields twice lured Robert W. Waterman to California before he finally bought a mine near Julian and went on to become governor in 1887. Above Right: This 1888 promotional advertisement for Oneonta, proclaiming the community to be the most desirable in the country, appeared just before the real estate economy collapsed.

The Boom and the Bust

103

Top: The Middletown School
dominates the other structures in
this 1898 photograph, which includes Jorres wharf and visages

of North Island and Point
Loma. Above: Shade trees and
low brush helped hold down the
dust from the still unpaved
streets of Davis's New Town,
circa 1890. Cargo was conve-
niently unloaded at the Spreckels

wharf, background, and shipped
to the nearby lumber and lime
companies.

Above: The view from Coronado to San Diego in 1888. A few months after this photograph was taken, palms and orange trees were planted along the grassy length of A Street and track was laid for the streetcar. In this early period, however, many of the houses were still roofed with canvas tenting.
Left: Workmen pause during construction of the Hotel Arthur on Market Street. The hotel still stands today, nearly a century later.

The Boom and the Bust

While new buildings will continue to rise on the San Diego State University campus, few will surpass the grace of Hardy Tower. It remains the historic center of the campus, with an open-faced bell tower rising above twin columns on either side of a tiled archway.

CHAPTER 6

San Diego in Color

THE COMPOSITION in this kaleidoscope is characteristic of the glow of San Diego, the eighth largest city by population in the United States.

Hundreds of years ago, explorers and settlers were lured by the awesome natural beauty of the harbor, mountains, and valleys of this region. Since the arrival of those Europeans, a parade of confident and colorful adventurers have made their way by land and by sea to San Diego.

In more recent years, the beauty of the natural setting of the city has been intensified by design. Between the time the railroad arrived and the advent of the television — a short sixty years — people the world over have been drawn to the color ease, and warmth of the region. San Diego has managed phenomenal growth without obliterating the very aspects of the region that continue to attract residents and tourists in greater and greater numbers each year.

Growing communities, architecturally innovative buildings, planned recreational areas, and restoration projects like the Gaslamp Quarter have created a spectacular skyline. With continued controlled growth and planning, the color of San Diego will become more vivid and picturesque.

It would be impossible to describe San Diego accurately without color. San Diego is colorful—in its past, its people, and its setting. These color illustrations and photographs are but a sampling of San Diego's imagery, old and new.

Above: The U.S.S. Cyane *as painted by artist Carleton T. Chapman. The vessel was the first U.S. warship to enter San Diego Harbor, July 29, 1846. She was commanded by Captain Samuel Francis DuPont, who sent a detachment ashore to raise the American flag on the shores of the Mexican republic. Right: A lithograph of a painting of some Diegenos (sic) by Arthur Schott for the U. S. Department of the Interior Report on the U.S. and Mexican Boundary Survey made under the direction of the Secretary of the Interior by William H. Emory.*

Top: This diorama, which was formerly on exhibit in the Los Angeles County Museum of Natural History, depicts the arrival of Juan Rodriguez Cabrillo in San Diego Harbor on September 28, 1542. Cabrillo gave the name San Miguel to the area, but this and names of the other places he discovered were changed by later explorers. Left: Sketch of Mission San Diego done by Robert S. Williamson of New York, circa 1850.

San Diego in Color

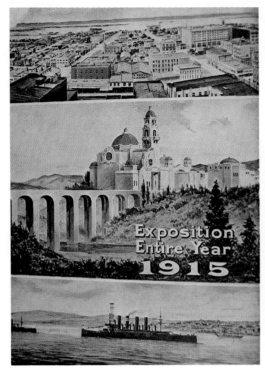

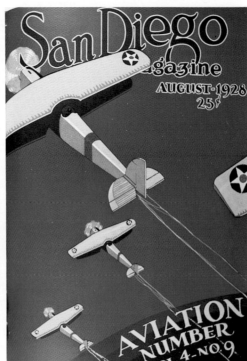

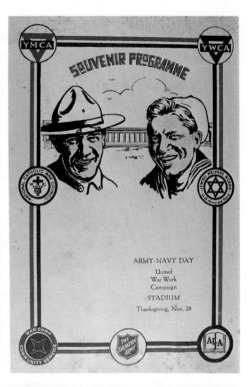

Collectable San Diego
memorabilia include (top, left to
right): an illustrated booklet issued
for the first Panama-California
Exposition; a 1928 edition of
San Diego Magazine selling for
twenty-five cents; and a program
recognizing a special Army-
Navy Day United War Work
Campaign celebrated in Balboa
Stadium. The agenda included
boxing, wrestling, a track meet
and a football game.

Opposite: Enchanting souvenirs continue with a cartograph of southern California advertising Western Air Express, a print of the scissors grinder who appeared on city streets until the 1930s, and (bottom) winsome bathers basking in San Diego's perpetual sunshine. Top Left: The Pacific Building

Company took the opportunity to advertise several of its developments in this promotion for the Garrick Theatre. Top Middle: The sectioned illustrations on the cover of this booklet, co-published by the Chamber of Commerce and the Panama-California Exposition, depict an idealized San Diego. Top Right: This pamphlet drew the population to Mission Beach.

Above Left: The print is one of several illustrations in a booklet entitled Our Navy, portraying the cruisers Newark and San Francisco. Above Right: The citrus packing box label dates to 1895, when A. Keen & Son delivered its first shipment to E. S. Moulton in Riverside.

San Diego in Color

The Reuben Quartermass-Louis J. Wilde residence at Twenty-fourth Street and Broadway was built in 1896. This Queen Anne Victorian residence was erected for Quartermass, a prominent businessman, and later became the home of Mayor Wilde. The domed circular tower and imposing classical corner entrance are the most distinguishing exterior features.

Opposite Top: The revitalized Balboa Theatre echoes the Spanish revival architecture of the Santa Fe Depot. The building was constructed in 1924.

Above Left: Ornamental lattice-work characterizes the restored Long-Waterman house on First Street.

Above Middle: In recent times, the Britt-Scripps house serves as a bed-and-breakfast inn. The two-story stained-glass windows distinguish the clean-lined Victorian.

Above Right: Situated a full story above street level, the Joseph F. Mumford residence features a remarkable harbor view.

San Diego in Color

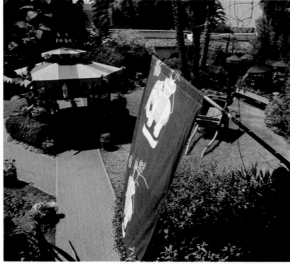

Top: Heritage Park hosts a gathering of historic landmarks which have become endangered elsewhere.

Above Left: A Mexican theme charms shoppers and diners in Old Town's Bazaar Del Mundo.
Above Right: Atmospheric gaslamps illuminate the treasures of

the Gaslamp Quarter National Historic District.

The whitewashed facade of the Mission San Diego de Alcalá punctuates the colorful Mission Valley landscape. As the first of the California missions, the structure has been undergoing restoration since the 1930s and today serves the community as a parish church in addition to attracting a tourist population.

The Coronado Bay Bridge (Top and Opposite Top), built in 1969, winds snakelike over the water, casting moody reflections which vary with the time of day. Above and Right: Patterned after Spanish originals, arched passageways and the famous Alcazar Gardens, here fronting the California Tower, grace Balboa Park. The gardens, planted for the 1935 Exposition, were restored in 1962 by the San Diego Rotary Club.

San Diego
An Illustrated History

116

Left: Although the Hotel del Coronado strikes up many legends of its own, it is the supposed meeting place of Prince Edward VIII, short-lived King of England, and Mrs. Wallace Simpson. Undoubtedly, more than a few romances have sprung from its turreted quarters.

San Diego in Color

Above: A stretch of blue water separates the city skyline from Shelter Island in this marina view taken from Point Loma. The juxtaposition of water and land provides a constant source of recreation for city dwellers. Right: Successful industry which has found a home in San Diego includes research and development, shipbuilding, defense, space-age technology, engine manufacturing and construction.

While a mounting population positions San Diego in the nation's top ten largest cities, environmentalists maintain that it is still one of the most desirable places to live. This moonlit view, as seen from Harbor Island, may be an indication why. Harbor Island, created by dredging in recent years, combines development of hotels, marinas and grassy recreational areas.

San Diego in Color

Adorned with turrets, cupolas and naturally finished hand-rubbed wood, the Hotel del Coronado is an exquisite example of Victorian architecture. Constructed in 1888, the hotel covers thirty-three beachfront acres and surrounds a one-and-a-half acre courtyard. The original five-story structure remains intact today, supplemented by a seven-story unit built in 1973, totaling seven-hundred guest rooms. The site is both a National Historic Landmark and a State of California Landmark.

CHAPTER 7

The World Sees San Diego

IF SAN DIEGO HAD leaned on Alonzo Horton in the last quarter of the nineteenth century, it would look to the leadership of John D. Spreckels at the opening of the twentieth century, for he brought a different focus to the city. Businessmen agreed when he spoke of the connection of the harbor to commercial sea traffic, the meaning of tidelands in terms of real estate, and the need for highways to bring traffic in and out of the city.

The Spreckels interests built theaters, ferryboat systems, workingmen's hotels, and even landscaped the City of Coronado. In 1906, Spreckels secured a railway to the east, and the San Diego and Arizona Railway was incorporated with construction beginning in 1908.

Spreckels's ownership of *The San Diego Union* and *The Evening Tribune* was perfect for promoting the city. Indeed, he would change the village to a city. Besides Spreckels though, there were other men who worked to solve the city's problems.

William Ellsworth Smythe, better known for having published the first *History of San Diego*, by the 1890s had begun a crusade for irrigation based upon his taste of droughts in Nebraska and New Mexico. In 1891 he founded the magazine *Irrigation Age* where he wrote that "irrigation was the biggest thing in the world." He wrote books including *The Conquest of Arid America*, and organized a National Irrigation Congress which became his forum.

Mrs. Tingley is joined by her counsellors at the Theosophist Institution on Point Loma in 1900. They called their institution "The Home for the Revival of the Lost Mysteries of Antiquity." Katherine A. Westcott Tingley, the theosophist crusader, came to San Diego in 1900 and was known as the "Purple Mother." She was the foundress and president of the International Brotherhood League and built an impressive series of buildings for her crusade.

He believed that aridity was a blessing, forcing people to cooperate, and that it had been no accident that many of the great civilizations had developed in lands of low mean rainfall. His efforts emphasized the precarious lack of water in the region.

The shortage of water had long since been a problem. A number of privately owned water companies provided what was required in different parts of the county. The Otay Water Company, incorporated in 1886, acquired by Spreckels in 1895, became the Southern California Mountain Water Company. In time city dams and reservoirs held emergency supplies.

In 1901 the California Development Company brought water into the Imperial Valley by diverting water from the Colorado River, an occurrence which would lead to many such diversions. Eventually, long and complex court proceedings would take place involving the diversion of waters. Several state governments and the federal government became involved in the determination of how various states would receive their fair share.

Top: Progressive farm hands bailed hay with this Auto-Fedan Hay Press. The picture was taken sometime after April 23, 1900, the date of the patent for this machine.

Above Left: The City Guard Band, circa 1900, had been playing about fifteen years when this photo was taken. Like many frontier cities, San Diego sponsored weekly concerts, usually celebrated at a bandstand in the town plaza. At the slightest excuse, the group performed all styles and types of music of the times.

Above Right: The State Normal School was an idea that took hold in 1894 with much negotiation at the local and state levels.

Competition for location of the school came from Pacific Beach, Coronado, Spreckels Heights, and University Heights. In 1897, the campus site in University Heights had been purchased for $18,500.

Above: Alpine, a community thirty miles east of San Diego, nestles in the pine trees of the Laguna Mountains. This photograph, taken at the Alpine Tavern circa 1910, shows the Lakeside to Julian stage which continued to run for another decade until the automobile made it obsolete. The mud wagon, as comfortably as could be expected, carried passengers, mail and luggage. Middle: These young Vaqueros were members of the Northern Diegueño, living and working on 120 acres of the Mesa Grande reservation. The land was established in 1893. Above Right: Miguel Lieras, a laborer, and his two children posed proudly for their photo in 1904, perhaps for some special occasion. Opposite: A 1904 photo of "Old Rosaria of Cienga San Felipe of Pala."

In the summer of 1901 and just two years later, the City of San Diego bought all the water systems within the city limits.

On August 14, 1906, at the University Heights reservoir, the water furnished by the Southern California Mountain Water Company to the city was turned on. An impressive ceremony brought the mountain water from the Otay Reservoir. For a while longer the "sunshine clubs" and the Chamber of Commerce would continue to overlook the fact that Southern California was a desert — an arid environment. And they well knew that here was a region with less than twenty inches of rainfall per year. Without help from neighboring regions, San Diego would be in trouble.

Another community leader who had an idea he always shared with others was George White Marston. He arrived from Wisconsin in 1870 and eight years later started his own company. Marston wanted San Diego to realize the feeling of achievement, to be what other large cities had not been. In 1907 he brought John Nolen, noted architect and planner of Cambridge, Massachusetts, to San Diego. His message was clear — to hold on to the beauty and space, the inexhaustible source of commercial and aesthetic wealth.

Of the city he said:

The scenery is varied and exquisitely beautiful. The great, broad quiet mesas, the picturesque canyons, the bold line of the distant mountains, the wide hard ocean beaches, the great Bay, its beauty crowned by the islands of Coronado; the caves and coves of La Jolla, the unique Torrey Pines, the lovely Mission Valley — these are but some of the features of the landscape that should be looked upon as precious assets to be preserved and enhanced . . .

The World
Sees San Diego

125

The Villa Montezuma, at the corner of Twentieth and K streets in Golden Hills, was built in 1887 for Jesse Francis Shepard, San Diego's most celebrated artist, writer and musician of the time. His architecturally and artistically unique, four-level home, photographed here in 1905, became the local center of culture when its bachelor occupant was not wandering the world.

Nolen returned in 1925 and made other visits. He advocated open space, ventilation, the development of parks and recreation, parkways and playgrounds. He pointed out that the city had not taken advantage of its natural resources. The designers, Nolen said, should have looked at cities like Seville, where because of the topography each street had a unique character. His views of San Diego touched the hearts of those who knew the city, but the recommendations he made brought little action by businessmen and city officials. Before long commercial buildings occupied space Nolen had hoped would be graced with public buildings and malls.

By the end of the year 1906, San Diego experienced another rise in real estate values when large-scale immigration came to Southern California. The "tourist trade" had been nurtured with hopes it would become a major economic source.

In that year the Spreckels interests acquired a number of buildings downtown and planned construction of other hotels and commercial structures making Broadway the major thoroughfare as Horton had envisioned.

In 1908, at a time the city could have worked toward the plans which Nolen had proposed, G. Aubrey Davidson, president of the San Diego Chamber of Commerce, and others realized that the opening of the Panama Canal could make San Diego into the major port on the west coast. Business leaders forged ahead with a plan to create a Panama-California Exposition to celebrate its opening, and in that way draw international attention to the city.

At that time eight-room homes cost four thousand dollars; a five-room bungalow was fifteen hundred dollars — twenty-six dollars down and twenty-six a month.

Top: By 1910 a long era of building ornate Victorian style residences slowed as Mission style became the favorite. Here, however, are examples of the fancy-grilled architectural styles popular in 1904. Above Left: The San Diego Historical Society has restored and opened the Villa Montezuma to the public. Above Right: In 1906 the home of pioneer Sierra Club member Charles P. Douglass stood at 202 Nutmeg Street.

The World
Sees San Diego

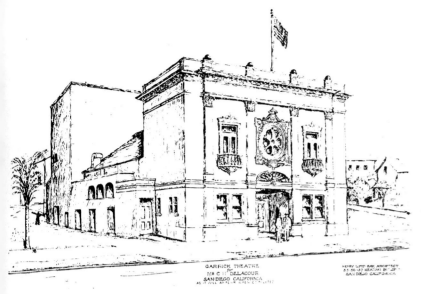

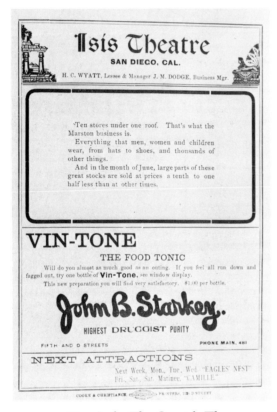

Top Left: The Garrick Theatre, designed in 1907 by Henry Lord Gay, was declared as San Diego's foremost dramatic play-house. Top Right: A chemistry class in session at Escondido Union High School. Above Left: An Isis Theatre program of June 11, 1904. Above Right: This morning scene was taken in 1910 at the yards of the Escondido Lumber Hay and Grain Company.

But not all residences of this era sold at that price. Some mirrored the flamboyant Victorian times, and new construction became a goal for San Diegans who wanted to be in tune with the dawn of a new era. Homes with views to the sea, balconies, peaked roofs, cupolas, and garish styles dotted the hillsides. A romantic evocation of the simple style of architecture characteristic of the city's heritage was produced in the California Mission Revival style. This style affected building plans for the Panama-California Exposition which made parts of the city a gilded reflection of a mythical past.

San Diego prepared for the great influx of people and commerce which the opening of the Panama Canal would surely bring. In 1911 the State of California relinquished control of the tidelands

to the City of San Diego on condition that the city raise $1 million through a bond election for development of the port. In 1912 the city did just that and in 1914 voted another $400,000. A thirty-foot channel was dredged into the harbor to the foot of Broadway, and the Broadway Pier, eight hundred feet long, became San Diego's first reinforced concrete pier.

City fathers estimated that 350,000 people in southern Italy and Russia alone had booked passage to San Diego by 1911.

On July 19, 1911, the exposition groundbreaking ceremonies took place. One dignitary parked his own new 1912 Flanders Touring Car, which a celebrity remarked had sold for one thousand dollars F.O.B., San Diego, fully-equipped.

City planners began to look about to make sure that their city

The U.S.S. Chicago, authorized by Congress in 1883, was one of the "protected ships," painted white and publicized by the navy as part of the White Squadron. The Chicago was the largest of the four vessels, the "A,B,C,Ds," Atlanta, Boston, Chicago and smaller Dolphin. She displaced 4,500 tons, steamed at eighteen knots and carried four eight-inch and fifteen five-inch guns.

The World
Sees San Diego

129

The Pioneer Hook and Ladder Company was the city's first fire department, established May 17, 1869. Three years later the San Diego Fire Engine Company No. 1, also a hook-and-ladder company, was organized. Advances brought salaries to the firemen in 1889, motorization between 1910 and 1916 and the William Kettner fireboat in 1918.

would have a pleasing appearance to visitors. The downtown area left without attention would have given an unpleasant impression to tourists coming from all parts of the world. Certainly it would not have been good for such places as the Pacific Squadron Hall, Ida Bailey's, Mamie Goldstein's, the Canary Cottages, and the Seven Tubs of Blood Saloon to stay open.

The council ordered the police department to begin a cleanup. In turn the job fell to the health department to make inspections, and most of the red-light Stingaree District was closed down.

Building in the downtown area became more active than at any other time in the city's history as blocks were rebuilt and structures changed to suggest the flavor of Spain, Hispanic America, Panama, and the influences of those regions on San Diego. Theaters such as the Cabrillo, Aztec, Alhambra, California, and later the Balboa represented examples of the trend.

The U.S. Post Office and Customs House had been designed in Mission Revival style by architects of the U.S. Treasury Department in Washington, D.C., and was dedicated in April 1913.

In June 1914, construction began for the new Santa Fe Railroad Station, built in that same symbolic style of Hispanic California.

At midnight on January 1, 1915, in Washington, D.C., President Woodrow Wilson pushed a button to light the grounds of the

Top: This 1910 photo showing
the San Diego ferryboat house,
restaurant, barber shop, ship's
chandlery and grocery store was
taken near the present site of the
San Diego Police Station and
Seaport Village.

Above Left: These fully-garbed
bathers gathered at the surf at
Coronado Beach in 1910. The
location appears to be just east of
the Hotel del Coronado.
Above Right: In the early days
of auto races held at the Lakeside
track, drivers such as Barney
Oldfield circled the field in the

spectacular new machines. Here
Oldfield appears in the "Green
Dragon," photographed
April 1907.

The World
Sees San Diego

131

Panama-California Exposition. The World's Fair opened in San Diego and San Francisco as the two cities held expositions to celebrate the completion of the Panama Canal. Each city had agreed that San Francisco would host a world's fair and San Diego would specialize in Pan-American themes centered on the Southwest.

In 1917 the exposition closed after having been extended for a year, leaving San Diegans some outstanding architectural beauties, and many people who had come to visit decided to stay.

While the exposition had been a great success, it was only a temporary enterprise. Civic groups working with the federal government before the turn of the century had given new meaning to the city when a military reservation was built and named for the hero of Murfreesboro, Major-General William Starke Rosecrans. The government gave other signs of interest in San Diego by the creation of the U.S. National Cemetery and the U.S. Navy Coaling Station on Point Loma.

The appearance of President Roosevelt's "Great White Fleet," in the Coronado Roads on April 13, 1908, did no harm in showing what an opportunity San Diego had to become a major naval base. The President had sent the fleet of sixteen vessels and sixteen thousand men around the world in part as a goodwill gesture, but more as a show of strength. The city celebrated as it had never celebrated before.

Opposite Top: America's La Mesa Studio distributed "Bonita of El Cajon" and later "Fifty Mile Auto Race" at Lakeside. Producer and director Allan Dwan, shown here, brought many of his films south of Hollywood for location shooting. Opposite Left: "Bronco" Billy Anderson was one of the many silent film stars working for a variety of motion picture companies. Opposite Right: The extraordinary Lakeside Inn, shown here in 1911, was used periodically as a movie set from 1911 to 1915. Above Left: The ferryboat Benicia unloaded passengers from the mainland to Coronado. Above Right: This advertisement exhibited San Diego's eagerness to draw some of Hollywood's cinema activity.

The World Sees San Diego

133

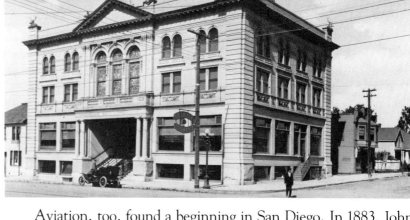

Top: A picnic gathering of the Mission San Diego Catholic Society in 1913 fronts the, as yet, unrestored church. Above Left: An AT & SF engine delivers passengers to the old depot in Del Mar, circa 1912. The name of the town was inspired by the poem "Paseo Del Mar" by Bayard Taylor. Above Right: The Elks Building at Broadway and Second Street.

Aviation, too, found a beginning in San Diego. In 1883, John J. Montgomery soared six hundred feet over Otay Mesa in a homemade glider, making man's first controlled winged flight.

In 1910 Glenn W. Curtiss established a flying school on North Island when Spreckels leased him land. Curtiss invited army and navy officers to receive flight instruction.

The first permanent U.S. Marine detachment moved to North Island in 1914. Three years later the army established the first aviation field at Imperial Beach renaming the post for Major William Roy Ream, the army's first flight surgeon who had been killed in an aircraft accident. The U.S. Armed Forces regard this as the helicopter capital of the world.

Left: Dedication of the fountain in Horton Plaza also marked the opening of the U.S. Grant Hotel on October 15, 1910. The plaza, donated by Alonzo Horton and designed by architect Irving Gill, became a focal point downtown. Kate Sessions, noted horticulturist, planted palm trees in 1895, and banker Louis Wilde contributed $10,000 to finance the fountain modeled after the Caragic Monument of Sysicrates in Athens and decorated to represent San Diego history.

These two panoramas, taken in 1912, portray San Diego three years before the Panama-California Exposition. Architecturally, styles were between the Victorian and Mission Revival eras. The views approximate the Gaslamp Historic District, where many fine turn-of-the-century buildings are being preserved.
Right:
Irving John Gill, one of San Diego's most noted historical architects, arrived in the city in 1894, after completing work on the Columbian Exposition in Chicago. For the next forty years, he worked in the region.

136

Opposite Top Left: "Blood encrusted junk, historic smuggler and pirate ship" lured visitors to the centuries old Ning-Po, moored as a tourist attraction at the foot of Market Street in 1913. She left San Diego that same year and is alleged to have been sunk off Catalina Island, Venice and other points along the coast. Opposite Top Right: Circa 1913, immigrants discovered a better way of life in San Diego.

Opposite Middle: Both stylish and functional in design, the Pacific Coast Steamship Company warehouse stood at the foot of Fifth Street. The photograph was taken in 1913. The structure was demolished in 1958. Opposite Below Left: San Diego's Architectural Association was depicted in The San Diego Union January 1, 1913. Active in both revitalization and planning, the group hurried the transformation of a village into a city. Opposite Below Right: The international headquarters of the Universal Brotherhood and Theosophical Society was organized and managed by Katherine Tingley.

These three peace officers, photographed in 1911, had checkered careers in San Diego law enforcement. Jefferson Keno Wilson (right), served as chief for four terms in his 25 years with the department. He began his career in Oceanside in 1886, was appointed a U.S. Deputy Marshall for San Diego County and later a customs inspector at Campo prior to his term with San Diego. He died in 1934 at the age of 71.

The World
Sees San Diego

137

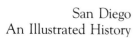

Top: The interior of the Santa
Fe Railroad Station Depot appears much the same today as it
did shortly after its opening.

North Island which had been a temporary naval station for four years became a permanent army air facility in 1915. Rockwell Field which occupied the south half of the island was named for Louis C. Rockwell, a second lieutenant. The Spreckels Company sold part of North Island to the Army Air Service, a branch of the Signal Corps, and in 1917 the government paid the Spreckels Company six million dollars for the entire North Island, at which time it became a Naval Air Station Command.

After April 6, 1917, when the United States declared war on Germany, the military presence became magnified. Soldiers who trained at Camp Kearny on the mesa north of Mission Valley later fought in the trenches of France.

The U.S. Destroyer Base, established in 1922, was developed after the navy reclaimed the mud flats and dredged the channel. During World War II the base became the U.S. Naval Repair Base and after the war was redesignated as the U.S. Naval Station.

Concerted community efforts answered the call to assist the military during wartime by negotiating for space for military establishments. The city gave the U.S. Navy 79 acres of submerged tidelands near present Marine Corps Replacement Depot and raised funds to buy 135 acres of privately-owned adjacent land to go with the other parcel.

If any force had worked in the 1910s to the benefit of the city, it was through this federal-local government and metropolitan-military complex relationship. The value of the armed forces became very clear to a community that had periodically held up the services to question — the military had real value not only for service to the country but also in terms of economic worth returned to the community.

Opposite Left: Representing the first train at Campo, September 16, 1916, over the San Diego and Arizona Railroad (left to right): John F. Forward, Sr., who as mayor of San Diego in 1909 broke ground for the railroad; John D. Spreckels, pioneer builder and financier of the railroad; Alphonso D. Grigsby and "Uncle" Lee Morris, pioneer settlers at Campo; and Harry L. Titus, chief counsel for Spreckels Companies and San Diego and Arizona Railroad Company. Opposite Right: A view of the tiled dome of the Santa Fe Depot in 1915. Above: Included in the National Register of Historic Places, the Santa Fe Depot reminds San Diegans of their mission heritage. The photos were taken shortly after the depot's opening.

The fishing industry, which had been important to San Diego from the 1860s as Chinese fishermen worked the waters off the coast, began to take hold. The Portuguese colony had begun in 1876. Its residents came directly overseas or via Gloucester, Massachusetts.

The Italians came largely from Sicily or Genoa, and their names first appear in the city directories around the turn of the century. Their colony and residential district along India Street remains an important and colorful example of an ethnic neighborhood linked to the larger community.

In 1917, shortly after they began to arrive from San Pedro, the Japanese introduced the long pole to the industry. It proved a more effective way to catch tuna than with seines.

Canneries established in 1909 expanded the business, but not until canned fish became significant to the diet during World War

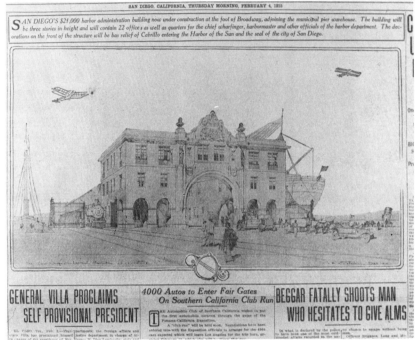

SAN DIEGO'S $21,000 harbor administration building now under construction at the foot of Broadway, adjoining the municipal pier warehouse. The building will be three stories in height and will contain 22 offices as well as quarters for the chief wharfinger, harbormaster and other officials of the harbor department. The decorations on the front of the structure will be bas relief of Cabrillo entering the Harbor of the Sun and the seal of the city of San Diego.

GENERAL VILLA PROCLAIMS SELF PROVISIONAL PRESIDENT

4000 Autos to Enter Fair Gates On Southern California Club Run

BEGGAR FATALLY SHOOTS MAN WHO HESITATES TO GIVE ALMS

I, and improved techniques and refrigeration came into being, did tuna become so vital to the American scene.

By 1917 some San Diegans bemoaned the lack of industry to bolster the economy. Others still saw San Diego as a green belt to be kept in perpetuity without the impact of heavy air-polluting industry. The election in 1917 for the mayoralty position gave Louis J. Wilde a victory over George White Marston in the colorful "Smokestacks vs. Geraniums" election. Although Wilde won the contest, Marston's visions of the city beautiful staved off industrial development.

As early as 1897 the Thomas Edison Company had a crew of cameramen in California shooting footage of various towns. In February 1898, they shot "Street, Scene San Diego," consisting of twenty-five feet of film of downtown San Diego. Between 1910 and 1925, twelve motion picture film companies built studios in the

Top: The U.S.S. Dreadnaught. Above Left: Giant turtles await shipment on the wharf, circa 1900. Above Right: As reported in The San Diego Union, *February 4, 1915: "San Diego's $21,000 harbor administration building now under construction at the foot of Broadway, adjoining the municipal pier warehouse."*

The World
Sees San Diego

Top: The Pollard Players gathered at Balboa Park to honor the screen stars during the first Panama-California Exposition. Above Left: Early environmentalists Ed Fletcher, George White Marston and John Nolen toured much of the back country to fully understand San Diego's potential for growth and beauty. Above Right: The seventeenth birthday celebration of Gathern P. Perry, in honor of the Acme Social Club, March 1, 1917.

San Diego area. Studio chiefs extolled the weather and the varieties of scenic backgrounds. The Siegmund Lubin studios in Coronado had indoor and outdoor stages including a castle. Other companies such as the American Flying "A", Essanay, Ammex, Nestor, Dudley, Pollard Company, S&L, and Grossmont studios located themselves in Lakeside, La Mesa, and the South Bay area.

Between 1915 and 1930, another twenty-five film companies used Balboa Park for shooting films. Some of those companies were the Famous Players Corporation, Pathe Exchange, Inc., San Diego Cinema Corporation, Vitagraph, Warner Brothers, Universal Film and Metro-Goldwyn-Mayer.

After this time, with the concentration of studios in the financial centers to the north, the only impact of film production in San Diego came when other studios returned here to film on location.

Above: Mary Pickford joined a motion picture company on location in Mission Valley, circa 1916. She was frequently on location in San Diego between 1915 and 1928. Left: Looking west on Broadway from Fifth Street, with Horton Plaza on the left, the sectioned photograph distorts the facade of the U.S. Grant Hotel. Aircraft were added to the picture for special effect.

The World
Sees San Diego

143

Top Left: The Russia and Brazil buildings housed but two of the cultural exhibits which were part of the Panama-California Exposition, 1915-1916.

Top Right: Spanish Colonial architecture was selected to represent the Hispanic focus of the Exposition. Shown here are the Plaza de Panama and El Prado.

Above: In the plaza central of Balboa Park, the U.S. Navy drilled and performed for thousands of visitors to the first Panama-California Exposition.

At the close of the decade sea commerce and highway transportation had not yet developed. The aviation industry had not yet blossomed. Only a few short years before, the town had little industry and relied on commercial fishing and agriculture. Now the city had a burgeoning military complex, a rail line to the hinterlands and, as Shelly Higgins wrote, "What an exciting place it was! There was so much doing, so much yet to happen."

On November 15, 1919, after twelve years and eighteen million dollars, John D. Spreckels drove the symbolic spike to mark the opening of the San Diego and Arizona Railway. The significance of the line hit the city when, following its arrival, "Transcontinental Railway Week" was declared. That began with Harbor Day on December 2, 1919, to highlight the value of San Diego's superb land-locked harbor as an outlet for the new railroad. Seventy-one warships at anchor in the harbor helped play a major role in the drama. The celebration hosting twenty thousand people ended at El Centro to symbolize the link between the interior and the coast connected by the railroad.

Many of the richly embellished structures on the Plaza de Panama were replicas of others existing throughout the Hispanic world. These built for the exposition, of course, were only shells, and by 1935 only a fraction of them remained.

The World
Sees San Diego

Cantaloupe packers posed for this photograph taken at the California Owl Brothers plant in El Centro circa 1930. Commercial agriculture grew rapidly in the San Diego area after the opening of major roads and railways to the east and refrigeration and storage facilities were improved. Immigrants from all over the world came to find stable jobs in the year-round business of farming.

CHAPTER 8

Between the Wars

IN THE UPCOMING decade agriculture would come into its own. From the Mexican border to Los Angeles, the valleys west of the Laguna Mountains flourished with avocado groves, fields of flowers, and lemon, orange and citrus trees.

The Imperial Valley and South Bay areas produced a wealth of grains, vegetables, fruits, and poultry products which opened new vistas for farmers and transporters.

The railroads had helped as did the storage of produce by refrigeration. San Diego's business leaders turned to highway transportation routes to the east to bring in farm products.

In November 1923, the city became the terminus of the Lee Transcontinental Highway, an all-weather route from the east. Another paved highway linked San Diego to Los Angeles. San Diego firms responded by construction of warehousing facilities near the Santa Fe depot and wharves.

The major roads brought thousands of immigrants seeking the good life.

John D. Spreckels maintained that to develop a city's commercial and industrial property with a ruthless disregard for its beauty was a policy only less shortsighted and fatal than to attempt to develop its beauty at the expense of its prosperity. He refused to see any necessary conflict between beauty and business.

In 1923, at the Hotel del Coronado he expressed his belief and faith in San Diego, but observed that "San Diego always just misses the train—and it's due to lack of cooperation."

Many San Diegans came out to witness the arrival of the first San Diego and Arizona train at the Santa Fe Depot. Among those aboard the historic ride were (left to right) William D. Stephens, governor of California, John D. Spreckels and Thomas E. Campbell, governor of Arizona. Others participating included Admiral Hugh Rodman, commander of the Pacific fleet, Louis J. Wilde, mayor of San Diego, and Brigadier General Joseph H. Pendleton, U.S. Marine Corps.

In planning for the greater San Diego, by 1921 the city government had reserved and improved thirteen parks; after Balboa Park in size were Torrey Pines Park, Soledad Park, and Collier Park. A playground commission employed twenty-five people who maintained the park system. Municipal golf links, baseball grounds, and city playgrounds encouraged people to move to San Diego. At the old exposition grounds in Balboa Park, a camp ground for automobilists had been established by the city. Here tourists flocked in increasing numbers to the twenty-acre campsite with running water, electric lights, wood for fires, and tables for picnics.

In 1921 real estate fell below the boom peak of 1912. Realtor Oscar Cotton wrote in his book *The Good Old Days* of real estate construction between 1925 and 1927. At that time La Jolla Hermosa, the La Jolla Beach and Yacht Club, Rancho Santa Fe, and other areas were impeccably designed and opened with grand advertising.

Throughout this decade construction was geared to opening up new areas of the city, especially East San Diego, with residential dwellings and commercial buildings in the downtown area replacing many of the older structures.

Downtown the new California Theatre building, the Medico-Dental Building, and the Bank of America (Spreckels Building) all graced the skyline.

Along San Diego's "Main Street" — Broadway — had been built a number of office structures and theaters which catered to tourists and U.S. Navy personnel. To enhance the Broadway entrance in 1926, a $1 million pier was added at the foot of "B" Street; later a pier costing $450,000 was completed at the foot of Broadway. Citizens wholeheartedly supported the investments in the city's growth.

Voters approved the construction of a new civic center on the tidelands, at a place engineers predicted an earthquake would cause the structure to sink into the sand and the bay, but this site, too, lay distant from the downtown area.

People got off the boats or trains and made their way by streetcar or taxi up Broadway to the major hotels and to the area which by 1930 would become the center of the financial and business district, Fifth Street and Broadway.

In East San Diego miles of streets were graded, sidewalked, and curbed. By 1921 University Avenue had been paved for 1.5 miles. Sagebrush lots that sold in this area in 1905 for $100, by 1911 brought $1,000; a seven-room home could be acquired for $5,800.

Vitagraph Motion Picture Company, which had come to San Diego about 1915, brought its crews to the Kensington area along the edge of Mission Valley, for it is an area surrounded on three sides by valleys and canyons. There they built a ghost town with Victorian houses and saloons for the backdrop of films.

Close by in Talmadge Park, Joseph Schenk subsidized and promoted *Movie Girl Subdivision* in 1925. In one of the units, streets were given the names of Norma, Constance, and Natalie Talmadge. To promote the area of Talmadge Park, Schenk brought the sisters from Hollywood via the train; they were then driven with their guests through Balboa Park to the subdivision.

The day the park was dedicated a rainstorm hit the city; William S. Hart's chaps and spurs got muddy, Buster Keaton (who was married to Natalie Talmadge) was soaked while riding in an open car, a promotion tent caved in crushing the dedication cake, and the three sisters, wearing flapper dresses and cloche-type hats decorated with jet beads, were drenched. Nonetheless the opening was a success and a credit to Hollywood.

Spreckels developed Mission Beach, later called Belmont Park, in 1925. The Mission Beach Ballroom was designed by architect Lincoln Rogers and built by Wurster Construction Company. The Spanish Colonial style building cost $2.5 million and became one of the main attractions of the amusement center. During World War II the pavilion would be the home of many big bands.

At Mission Beach a bath house which covered 2.5 acres and cost $450,000 had fifteen hundred dressing rooms. Spreckels thought that this would stand as another monument to his love for his adopted city.

This drawing of the city in 1921 by Frank H. Brown, landscape and industrial artist, proved remarkably detailed and accurate when compared with photographs and fire maps. The rendering appeared in The San Diego Union *May 21, 1921.*

Between the Wars

The San Diego Military Barracks were built prior to the Civil War and used intermittently until 1898. At that time an artillery battery moved from the old barracks to the newly constructed Fort Rosecrans, leaving the structure largely unoccupied until its demolition in 1921. A parking lot marks the old site today.

San Diego
An Illustrated History

Not all his projects received approval. He proposed construction of a bridge to Coronado in 1926. Reluctant voters rejected the idea.

Then Spreckels, who had seen the emergence of a city he had helped to achieve prominence, passed away in 1926. Spreckels made contributions to the city's growth that are unlikely to be equaled again by one man. With his death came the end of a legend.

Colonel Ira C. Copley bought *The San Diego Union* and *The Evening Tribune* in 1928 and directed the papers until he passed away in 1947. Then his son, James C. Copley who became the major philanthropist in San Diego after Spreckels, took over. James Copley died in 1973, and his wife Helen has managed and directed the role of the papers since that time.

When the first horse-racing track opened on January 1, 1916, San Diego and Tia Juana became partners in a relationship unique

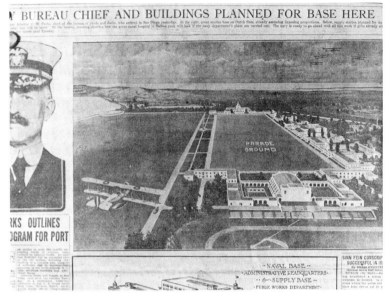

among U.S. border communities. Tia Juana started out as an escape hatch for vices not allowed in the United States. Mexico had allowed gambling since January 1, 1916, when horse racing and other sporting activities attracted exposition visitors.

The sophisticated two-million-dollar Agua Caliente resort, race track, golf course, bath house, plunge, and world-famous casino opened on June 23, 1928 — the whole system catered to the film colony and big spenders. Yet across the border in San Diego in 1930, the highest rate of bankruptcies in our nation beset the city.

October 30, 1929 was a historic day for the nation, remembered as the date of the stock market crash and the beginning of The Great Depression. Yet on November 9, 1929, Philip and Theodore Gildred opened their $2.5 million Fox Theater designed by William Templeton Johnson. That evening more than 30,000 people (out of San Diego's total population of 150,000) packed the streets to see the parade and a special trainload of stars and celebrities who had come on the Santa Fe for the event.

Though unemployment rose, some stability came as military spending continued to rise during the depression, and San Diego became known as a "sailor's town."

Income from agriculture reflected the county's second greatest source of money. As the major impact of the depression hit the city, people suffered: they lost homes, some personal fortunes vanished, and in San Diego property values dropped. But for all that, no one had to face the bleak cold winters, nor did many suddenly lose their jobs.

In Imperial Valley, families who had begun the migration to California camped by the side of irrigation ditches without shelter and became victims of disease and hunger. *Business Week* of July 3, 1931, estimated that thirty thousand families had entered Califor-

San Diegans got a glimpse of the military units to be constructed when renderings appeared in The San Diego Union *August 1, 1920. They included a perspective view of the Naval Training Station and Administrative Headquarters and Supply Base. The population unhesitatingly voted in favor of their city's strengthened partnership with the U.S. Navy.*

Between the Wars

Top: At the time it was designed by the Quayle Brothers, Balboa Stadium was the largest stadium of its kind in the world.

Middle: The ivy-covered walls of San Diego High School were razed to eliminate earthquake hazard.

Right: On a test run, Charles A. Lindbergh and the Spirit of St. Louis soared over Mission Beach. After Spreckels built the pavilion, an amusement center followed to match any on the coast.

nia from the "Dust Bowl," and reported that as one of the greatest interstate migrations since the California Gold Rush. In 1933 the U.S. Department of Agriculture estimated that eighty thousand out-of-state cars entered through Yuma; in its view, 1933 was the year the migration had begun. In February 1936, policemen from some west coast cities took up stations on the sixteen rail and highway arteries coming into California, Oregon, Nevada, and Arizona with orders to turn back people who had no definite reason for coming into California.

San Diegans used their inventive genius and found a variety of ways to muddle through the hard times. Young men paddled rafts around the bay with ice cream and candy bars packed in dry ice to sell to the sailors on board ships. At night on the bay side of

After his successful trans-Atlantic flight, Charles Lindbergh returned to San Diego on September 21, 1927. Sixty-thousand people packed Balboa Stadium to celebrate America's hero, who made it a point to visit the Mahoney plant to thank the builders of his plane.

Between the Wars

153

Opposite: Ocean villas in La Jolla were choice properties when Mrs. Mary Ashbough entertained in 1924 at 202 Sea Lane. Above: Architect Charles Quayle, resting here on a blueprint cabinet modified into a bed, and his father and brother were among the best known architects in Denver before they migrated to San Diego in 1900. Among Charles's designs are Balboa Stadium, the Elks Building and the Tioga Hotel. Left: Developer Joseph Schenk accompanied the Talmadge sisters to the opening of Talmadge Park in 1925. Promoted as the "Movie Girl Subdivision," the development boasted homes designed by architects of the stars.

Coronado beach, flashlights signaled Morse code to men on board destroyers who came in shore boats to trade bootleg booze for ships' stores. Others gathered scrap iron from vacant lots and damaged cars and sold it to be flattened and carried by ship to Japan.

Aviation flourished in the mild climate, and a number of experimental flights by civilian and military personnel took place. Newspapers carried accounts of non-stop and distance flights and of attempts to set speed records.

Commerical aviation took hold when Ryan Aeronautical opened in 1927 and inaugurated flights from San Diego to Los Angeles. Some other firms were Prudden-San Diego Airplane Company, Solar Turbines International, and Rohr Industries Inc.

Following the building of the *Spirit of St. Louis* by Ryan, one of the most cherished achievements of San Diegans, Charles A.

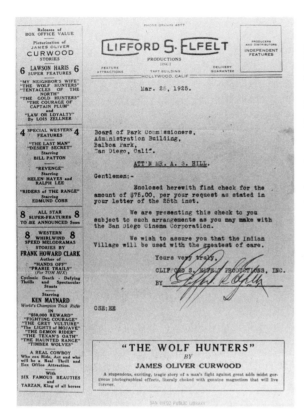

Above Left: A letter, dated March 25, 1925, from Clifford S. Elfelt Productions, sought permission to film within the Pueblo Indian Village in Balboa Park. The village, created during the first Panama-California Exposition, was used as a Boy Scout headquarters until the 1940s. Above Middle: Crowds flocked to Escondido for free grapes and to watch the annual crowning of the Grape Day Queen each summer. Here the Queen and Miss San Diego posed in 1927. The festival is no longer held. Above Right: The florid interior of the Pantages Theatre bore a religious motif. It has long since fallen to the wrecking ball.

Lindbergh flew to St. Louis, and then made his non-stop flight to Paris. In 1928, Lindbergh Field, made from reclaimed land, was dedicated for full operational service.

Earlier the lighter-than-aircraft U.S.S *Shenandoah* had visited the city, dropping mail sacks en route. In 1932, the U.S.S. *Akron* arrived from Lakehurst, New Jersey. An army-navy review was held in which more than four hundred aircraft flew over the city to demonstrate a hoped for awakening to the need for a stronger military arm in light of world-wide events.

The U.S. Marine Base, dedicated in 1919, mustered in the first marine recruits, and the Naval Training Command on the west end of the air field was commissioned on June 1, 1923. Rockwell Field and all of North Island had been given over to the navy for use as a principal air station. Ugly mud flats filled in along the bay became a recreation field for navy personnel.

Following Franklin Delano Roosevelt's election, the federal and local government interplay took place as it had in 1900–1920. The first New Deal became synonymous with "action," and to San Diegans that meant the Democrats giving a lift to an ailing nation. Roosevelt's attitude had been "Try Something," and soon the legislation took hold.

The channel of the harbor was widened, the airport enlarged, and a baseball park, Lane Field, was built at the foot of Broadway. Bill Lane, owner of the Hollywood baseball team in the old Coast League moved the franchise to San Diego. Today, at the foot of Broadway, a parking lot covers the ground, yet the roars can still

Fancy scrolls formed an arch over the entrance to the Pickwick Theatre, which was built under the direction of Louis J. Wilde on Fourth Street between Broadway and C Street in 1904. The theatre housed vaudeville and dramatic stock shows until it became a motion picture theatre. In time it was called the Pantages Theatre.

Workmen still toiled on the
polychrome tiled dome of the
Balboa Theatre days before its

grand opening in the early
1920s. The facade, designed
by William Wheeler, still lacks
statues or figures that were never

placed in the niches on the north
exterior wall.

San Diego
An Illustrated History

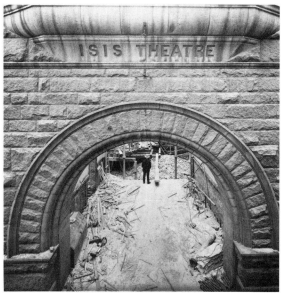

Above Left: Madame Ernest Schumann-Heink, renowned opera star, signs stock certificates for the 1935-1936 Exposition in this photograph which appeared at the same time. Above Right: The pain and the hurt at the loss of a friend. Left: Some of the best looking girls in town, shown here in 1930, performed nightly at the Hotel Douglas and Nite Club at Second and Market streets. Also known as the Creole Palace, the hotel was built by William McCloskey in 1924 for founders George Ramsey and Bob Rowe. They named the building for Frederick Douglass, humanitarian, abolitionist, writer and orator. The building was slated for demolition in 1981.

While several of the larger fishing vessels followed the meandering fish banks as far away as the Galapagos Islands, many fishermen expressed concern when the albacore, the principal catch of the tuna industry, shifted further out to sea. Survival in a competitive industry depended on a greater range of travel, and so a larger vessel. The photo above, taken about 1925 along the Pacific Highway, depicts the Italian community which arrived at the turn of the century and whose names appear in the city directories. Their colorful colony on India Street arrived either directly from the motherland or via Gloucester, Massachusetts.

"We Built the Ryan New York to Paris Plane"

be heard for the DiMaggio brothers, Ted Williams, Max West, Luke Easter, and Bobby Doerr. Hamburgers went five for a dollar, tickets for bleacher seating at fifty cents, and cold beer for twenty cents a large cup.

The U.S. Coast Guard Station with seaplane landing ramps and the present police station at Pacific Highway and Market Street, designed by the world famous Quayle Brothers and Albert Treganza, architects, are but a few of the Works Progress Administration buildings which stand as invaluable assets to the community.

Top: Workers responsible for the construction of the Spirit of St. Louis joined Lindbergh (seventh from left). Above: The U.S.S. Shenandoah is shown here a short time before her midair disintegration during a thunderstorm over Ohio in 1925.

Between the Wars

The famed Agua Caliente Resort and Race Track lured an impressive Hollywood clientele south of the border after its opening in 1928. Al Jolson, Babe Ruth and Jack Johnson were a few lulled by the mariachis and drawn to the gambling tables and ponies. In 1930 a $140,000 handicap was announced by Jim Crofton, resort manager, in Los Angeles and San Diego newspapers, attracting even greater trade to the Gold Room where the big money was won and lost. After Lázaro Cardenas became President of Mexico, he issued a decree on July 21, 1935, banning gambling and virtually eliminating the Agua Caliente from the scene.

Work had begun on the 1935 California-Pacific International Exposition in Balboa Park, helping to alleviate employment in the trades.

The WPA employed artists, musicians, historians, writers, archaeologists, and those in creative professions at a time when they became the first to be unemployed. Some of their work is found in libraries and post offices, in the murals and statues gracing San Diego's university campuses. State Normal School had been founded in 1897, became a state teachers college in 1921, and more recently San Diego State University, whose Aztec Stadium was built in part with WPA support.

Having employment, men began to regain their pride, and while wages remained quite low, so did food prices. Chicken and rabbit sold for 18¢ a pound, prime rib roasts 20¢ a pound, and roast pork was 12.5¢ a pound.

The depression bottomed out in 1934, but San Diego had not been an industrial city, therefore, there was no large layoff of

The interior of the stately Coronado home of newspaper publisher Colonel Ira Clifton Copley was photographed in 1932. Publisher of eleven newspapers in California and four in his native Illinois, Copley emerged from a pioneer farmer's family to a career as a utilities executive, congressman and, ultimately, newspaper publisher. He was one of the prime movers of San Diego to a city of prominence.

Between the Wars

Right: Children's Day at the Japanese First Congregational Church of San Diego, June 13, 1926. Earlier in the century, a large number of Japanese families moved to San Diego from San Francisco and established a community here. Its business center was located in the area of Fifth and Market streets.

The customs checkpoint into the United States, shown here at San Ysidro in 1925, causes delays while authorities check for goods or persons being transported into the States. By contrast, movement from the States into Mexico has always been quick.

workers. By 1935, a revival came in building, especially of tract housing, as immigrants continued to look for work in the year-round mild climates.

Boulder Dam, completed in 1935, assured water for the time being in the dry coastal regions. FDR delivered the dedication address for the city and county civic center building, while San Diegans recalled the Nolen Plan, which had truly influenced planning and development alongside the magnificent harbor. Others still hoped the rest of the President's ideas would take shape, but the war in Europe loomed large.

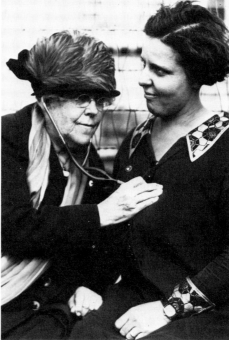

Top Left: Kensington was established in 1910 by G. Aubrey Davidson, who was commissioned by the Santa Fe Railway to find and develop a first-class residential district in the city.

Middle: Dr. Charlotte Baker was the first woman to serve as president of a county medical society in California. Top Right: Carrie Shannon, long-time beloved teacher, joined her class on

a field trip to Presidio Park.
Above: Although structural alterations have been proposed for La Jolla Cove, its natural setting almost defies change.

Laying the cornerstone at Del Mar on August 22, 1931, are Governor Frank Merriam, Frank McLauglin, Adolph Muchleisen and Bing Crosby. Above: Wartime scene at Camp Callan, December 1941. Middle: An electric bus in downtown San Diego. Opposite Top: A 1946 labor strike at a construction site.

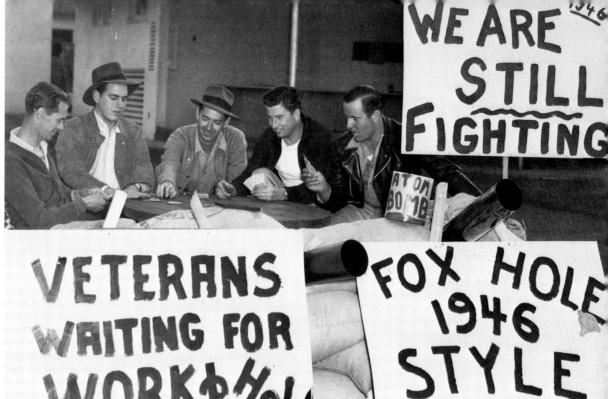

An enthusiastic supporter of the United States' participation in World War II throws Sunkist oranges to departing troops at Camp Callan on March 3, 1941.

On May 29, 1935, after new building and rehabilitation of the 1915 exposition buildings, the California-Pacific International Exposition opened in Balboa Park. At the opening of the fair, Franklin Delano Roosevelt visited the park and spoke to a capacity crowd at Balboa Stadium.

By September 1935, Reuben H. Fleet moved Consolidated Aircraft Corporation to San Diego from the snow fields of Buffalo and became a prime city employer in time to contribute heavily to the war effort. Later the firm merged with Vultee to become Convair. The mild climate, the availability of land, and the potential for expansion attracted the company. When such firms arrived, the rapid growth in population and military facilities helped to soften the depression and smooth out the economy.

Opposite Top Left: In a vivid display of air power the Navy flew 242 of its aircraft over the city on July 28, 1932. The photo depicts the U.S. Naval Air Station and the Naval Training Center buildings. Opposite Top Right: A summons mars a Fourth of July 1931 collision aftermath. Opposite Below: The "Humorous Map of El Cajon Valley," dated 1931. Above: Encinitas boasted its name in broad letters over the street, a custom in southern California cities in the 1920s. The coming of the railroad in the early 1880s marked the emergence of the sleepy resort town. Left: Dr. and Mrs. Albert Einstein arrived in San Diego on December 31, 1930, while on a pleasure voyage on the Belgenland. The awe in which he was held by others is clearly evident in the expressions of those around him, including Mayor Harry C. Clark's.

Between the Wars

169

Above: President Franklin Delano and Eleanor Roosevelt attended the dedication of the San Diego Civic Center on July 16, 1938, a date also marking the 169th birthday of the city. Right: Speaker Jean Rand confronted an agitated group during a Communist riot at Pantoja Plaza on Memorial Day 1933. A total of 300 Communists were known to have incited the riot, however, both the Union Tribune and the International Labor Defense criticized police action. All charges were dropped except for those against Frank Young, a black man convicted of simple assault, and he was fined $100 and given sixty days in jail.

Above Left: Grossmont resident Carrie Jacobs Bond was a song composer who had performed before Enrico Caruso and Presidents Theodore Roosevelt and Warren Harding. Above Right: When Californians sought a new lease on life during the Depression, many turned toward evangelists. Sister Aimee Semple McPherson preached the "Four Square Gospel" in a spectacular performance at her Angelus Temple in Los Angeles. Her principal address was titled "From Milk Pail to Pulpit" and she regularly ended her three-day pageant with a healing service. Left: By 1934 the U.S. Immigration and Customs Station had been upgraded considerably.

Yet across the border President Lázaro Cárdenas had banned gambling in Mexico and Agua Caliente; a drawing card for visitors to and through San Diego ended for a time.

The federal government continued to trickle money and hence jobs into the local market. In 1936 the exposition was extended for a year; WPA advanced funds to begin the Del Mar race track—a source of work and income for the entire state.

A sunny December 1929 photograph of Salvation Army workers posing before they begin their day's work. The organization, still active in the San Diego area, has its main offices on Seventh Avenue in downtown San Diego and continues to serve the community through its many charitable activities.

Top Left: A parade down Broadway, circa 1929. Top Right: A fashionable crowd attending the *dedication of the Serra Museum. Below Left: San Diego has long been a leader in design and manufacture of airplanes. Below Right: A night performance by the San Diego Symphony Orchestra in the* *Organ Pavillion at Balboa Park, circa 1938.*

Opposite Top: The Globe Theatre, a beautifully designed structure patterned after its British counterpart, is shown here after its completion as a feature of Balboa Park in the 1935-1936 Exposition. Left: A miniature village was constructed for the Exposition where visitors viewed midgets at work.

Top: The bands of Glen Miller, Artie Shaw, Benny Goodman,

Duke Ellington and the Dorsey Brothers played to overflow crowds at the Pacific Square Ballroom in the 1930s and 1940s. Today the structure houses county offices. Above: Babe Ruth, Carl Klindt and Lou Gehrig at Balboa Stadium, October 28, 1937. Klindt retired from baseball to become a Coronado policeman.

Top Right: Very likely, these ladies participated in a publicity stunt for the San Diego Zoo or the

Panama-California Exposition. The unidentified photograph is dated 1935. Above: The Pueblo Indian Village, shown here in 1935, had been built twenty years earlier and in time became a motion picture set, a locale for organized camping and, finally, a Boy Scout headquarters. The location was Park Avenue, just north of the present-day Zoological Society.

Above: A crushing crowd responded to a liquidation sale at Davidson's during the Depression. The establishment stood at 845 Fifth Street in the old Louis Bank of Commerce Building. Above Middle: Samuel and Fannie Friedhof operated this "streamliner" diner at 2521 Pacific Boulevard during the late 1930s, not too far from the aircraft plants working at full force in the pre-war years. Right: A world premiere at the Spreckels Theatre between Second and Third on Broadway.

Above: Attendants pose behind the polished counter of the Monarch Drug Store, southeast corner of Fifth and Broadway, about 1933. The menu advertising bacon and eggs for twenty-five cents and Silex brewed coffee for five cents lends some clues to a much different era. Left: On Friday, January 6, 1939, heavy swells from a northern storm rode one of the year's highest tides to send water surging against the shore in a spectacular and damaging display of sea power. Particularly hard hit was Mission Beach, top, where 400 sandbags protecting a home on Ocean Front Walk traveled a block during the onrushing tide. Ocean Beach, bottom, was also flooded, water surged over Ocean Boulevard in Coronado, and "Depression Town," a collection of shacks at the mouth of the Tijuana River below Imperial Beach, was swept away.

Between the Wars

Segregated Mexican families rented these ramshackle homes in the early 1940s. The landlord's home, in the background, was somewhat better maintained. Mexican immigrants found employment mainly in agriculture or on the railroads. The outbreak of World War II provided more jobs in war-related industries.

CHAPTER 9

San Diego Becomes a City

AT THE CLOSE OF the 1930s the census for the city was 203,321 and 289,349 for the county; in spite of the influx of immigrants from truly blighted and depressed regions, the population had not doubled. New problems, however, continued to plague the city — housing, traffic, pollution. One answer to San Diego and the Imperial Valley's lack of water came in 1940 with the dedication of the All-American Canal.

Before 1940 the city had changed slowly. Some persons clung to the theory that San Diego lacked industry as the viable economic base. Between the wars local business had catered to and become dependent upon the navy, the retired, and middle-class familes who made up the largest proportion of local residents.

Tourism remained a major souce of income, while agricultural production, aircraft manufacturing, and fish canning brought other revenues as the principal exportive industries. Food processing, printing, stone clay, glass, and iron and steel products were mainly for local consumption.

Between October 1939 and July 1941, food costs went up 12.5 percent, clothing 11.5 percent, rent and furnishings about 5 percent, but utilities decreased 4 percent; all the while housing in the city remained stable. There was a surplus of available residences after the major units of the Pacific Fleet moved to Pearl

179

Top: Streetcar lines characterize the view looking eastward along Broadway approximately 1940. Above: Linda Vista in 1940 looking north from an old olive orchard. In this scene most of the single-family residences were still in the framing stages of construction.

Harbor, but as workers flocked into San Diego, vacancies were taken up and a housing crisis occurred.

Government agencies erected eight thousand units, and private contractors built eighty-five hundred units as they competed to solve the problem.

Mission Valley was the site of a trailer camp with 650 units. Each rented for seven dollars a week. Laundries and toilets were communal, and families were limited to two children. Because of its prior experience with migrant workers, the Farm Security Administration was given responsibility for the camp.

A tent city also sprang up in Mission Valley, but no government agency would claim responsiblity. Three thousand homes were built on Kearny Mesa where the government tried a social experiment—rents were based on the renter's ability to pay rather than on the size of the house the family occupied.

When the Germans moved across France and the low countries in May 1940, France was beaten and Britain pushed off the continent. The Nazi war machine had been effective through the air. San Diego had four plants capable of producing military aircraft: Consolidated, Rohr, Ryan, and Solar. In light of European events, the British Royal Air Force, the American navy and war departments reacted by placing tremendous orders for warplanes with these San Diego companies thereby tripling the work force.

Above: During the war years this construction worker supported his mother, sister and niece in an unfurnished frame house which rented for twenty-five dollars a month. Left: The proprietor of this trailer court most likely provided an electric washing machine, for a fee, in addition to these rudimentary facilities.

The San Diego area became home to a wide variety of significant military installations with naval bases predominating. The major installations included the Eleventh Naval District Headquarters, United States Naval Training Center, North Island Naval Air Station, Miramar Naval Air Station, Marine Corps Recruit Depot and Camp Pendleton near Oceanside. The United States Navy took control of the waterfront and control of all shipping for security reasons. The impact of recruits for the armed forces alone pressed the city's services and made it clear that San Diego could never be the same small town again.

Thousands of immigrants came to San Diego to work in defense and war plants. They came mostly from the Middle West and

Top: As soon as agriculture flourished in the San Diego region, vendors arranged the backs of trucks to display the produce they had bought wholesale from the farmers. Above: These three young men joined thousands in the migration to San Diego to find work in an aircraft factory. They could expect wages of sixty-five cents an hour.

the Rocky Mountain region to earn 65¢ an hour in the aircraft industry; some advertisements promised as much as $135 a month plus overtime. The average work week at this time remained forty-four hours, but few people worked a normal week. The magnitude of the war effort, including the arrival of troops, brought every aspect of city and county services, from the police department to garbage collection, under stress.

Since the population increase was seen myopically by city officials as having been caused largely by federally induced problems, in their view the city should receive federal support to finance new water facilities, roads, highways, and schools. Even Consolidated Aircraft Corporation, until this time a small industrial plant managed locally, now became a giant industry, committed to assist in the defense of the nation.

Since the federal housing and certain war plants were federally owned, they were tax exempt and, therefore, did not add to the tax base.

With the approval of the President, the navy began emergency construction of an aqueduct to bring Colorado River water two hundred miles from the east to the city.

In 1941 with the unemployment picture improving and wages going up, labor disputes arose. Clashes between unions became as commonplace as they were between labor and management. San Diego had been an "open-shop" town but quickly became closed. Butchers, clothing workers, automobile servicemen, and welders went on strike along with lumber workers and building tradesmen.

Above: Consolidated Aircraft Corporation workers, picnicking at curbside in December 1940, were still smiling. Automobile and gasoline shortages had not yet hit the city and parking lots were still full. Left: A favorite gathering place was Geo's Amusement Place, owned and operated by George R. Webber, at 2044 India Street.

San Diego
Becomes a City

Above: On January 10, 1939, spectators watch with mixed feelings as the U.S. Navy displays its West Indies airplanes. Top: San Diego has long been host to a large number of military personnel. This photograph, circa 1926, shows a young sailor relaxing in the downtown YMCA.

The issues were varied, ranging from increases in pay of one dollar a day to management violations of contracts.

In the summer of 1941 a national magazine told how the defense boom had caused anxiety among San Diegans. Local planners asked, "What could the city do to accommodate the demand on public services required by this influx of new residents?"

Federal housing brought relaxed construction laws. Linda Vista, designed on four squares miles of flat mesa land, helped ease the housing crunch for servicemen and war workers.

At 10:05 A.M., on December 7, 1941, radio broadcasts were interrupted to describe the Japanese attack on Pearl Harbor. Officers were summoned back to their stations. Trucks rolled up Broadway with orders for servicemen to return to their ships or stations immediately.

In Balboa Stadium, the Bombers, San Diego's professional football team, lost to Los Angeles. Servicemen in attendance received refunds. By 2:00 in the afternoon *The San Diego Union* had an extra edition on the streets headlined "U.S. Fleet Battles Japs as Tokyo Declares War." A traffic jam developed on Harbor Drive as people stared at the warships in the bay. Some people, when told of the attack, asked, "Where *is* Pearl Harbor?"

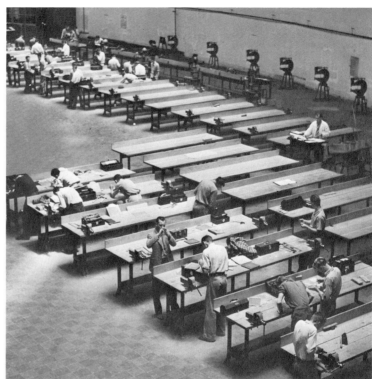

The harbor excursion boat *Silvergate* received instructions from a navy patrol boat to return to the dock; in haste the vessel ran aground and tourists had to be evacuated to shore. Private aircraft were grounded.

Twelve hundred ground observers manned sixty-one posts of the army's air-warning network throughout the county. Before the end of the year defense officials ordered blackouts in the city. Anti-aircraft guns appeared atop Consolidated, and aircraft spotters watched the skies from the tower in the Serra Museum and key points in Mission Hills.

Nets and a boom closed the entrance to the harbor. Enemy submarines attacked coastal shipping, but for a time the story made

Top Left: The completion of Linda Vista housing for war workers was welcomed, even if landscaping would be months away. Top Right: A vocational school at Consolidated Aircraft prepared students for the defense industry. Above: Palm trees enhanced the austerity of the Consolidated Aircraft Corporation building.

San Diego Becomes a City

Top Left: A Mexican family living near Logan Heights typically breakfasted on corn flakes and tortillas. Top Right: The Balboa Public School at 1844 South Fortieth Street was so crowded with children from construction, defense and military families that these second and third graders attended classes in the cafeteria. Above: Aircraft workers' wives hung laundry on the open plots adjacent to the trailers they called home during the war years. Farm Security Administration trailer camps sprung up in Mission Valley, Kearny Mesa and wherever else workers were able to get to the factories easily.

the rounds that if the Japanese wanted to bomb San Diego, they had only to fly to Tia Juana, still brightly lit, make a left turn and be over the city.

Green and brown camouflage netting covered the slope of Middletown hills above Consolidated Aircraft to the edge of the harbor. Once in a while the rubber outhouse and the livestock swayed with the breeze.

Every corner of the city and county had a military installation. Vessels carrying troops and supplies moved in and out of the harbor with frequency.

War plants operated around the clock; the city bustled as workers traveled from rented apartments to work, often on double shifts. Restaurants, tattoo parlors, the Hollywood Burlesque Theatre, and Bradley's 5 & 10 Saloon on Horton Plaza did a flourishing business. The building constructed in 1923 for the Stephens Investment Brokers Company in a Florentine Medici design still had the beautifully stenciled beams throughout the building. But now, in wartime, cheap facades covered over San Diego's historical past, and San Diego typified a city given over completely to the war effort.

In 1942 by virtue of a civilian exclusion order, all Japanese aliens and citizens living south of the San Dieguito River had to be removed from the region; a month later those from the north county left. The Western Defense Command transported some two thousand Japanese from San Diego to special reserves away from the coast.

During those years San Diegans put great effort into the war. After all, San Diego had been a military town; its residents were in part military; its sons had gone off to war; the retired military had remained here, and many had been called back to active duty. Buying necessities became difficult; certain luxuries disappeared altogether. The cost of living had not risen too much overall since 1939: a home with five rooms still sold for $4,750, a four-door Chevrolet for $998, and some entertainment could still be had, for there was, in spite of the conflict, a sense of activity and excitement.

Top: A real estate sign in May 1941. The Mission Hills stucco with three bedrooms and two baths would demand $252,500 forty years later. Above left: Streetcars were imaginatively converted into dwellings and equipped with electricity, running water and bathrooms. They rented for twenty-five dollars a month in 1941. Above Right: During the years just prior to and throughout World War II, many aircraft and construction workers and their families lived in tent cities.

San Diego
Becomes a City

187

Above and Opposite Left: Street parties erupted on VJ Day as San Diegans celebrated around the clock. Victory had special significance for the military port whose energies had been concentrated on the war effort for the past four years.

When the conflicts in Europe and Japan were over, bringing a halt to war contracts, a recession came to the city. Servicemen left, workers chose to return home, and unemployment rose.

Women, eased out by returning servicemen, had chinked the armor of business and industry by proving they could do almost any kind of work at all levels.

The *New York Times* reported late in 1947 that contracts had been cut for the aircraft industry, and that problems would arise for thousands of men and women seeking jobs. More significantly, these firms could not convert to peacetime markets. But San Diego did not experience the serious fallback which officials had predicted would take place because back in 1945 San Diegans had made plans to cope with anticipated shrinkage in the number of jobs when the war ended. Some imaginative plans for the vitalization of the city began to come anew from various civic, political, and business elements.

The approval of a bond issue to develop Mission Bay finally came right after the war, although the idea had been voiced by Glenn Rick in the late 1920s. In 1958 the city council adopted the master plan for the forty-six-hundred-acre Mission Bay Aquatic park after long and sometimes discouraging discussions. It is one of the most remarkable human recreation parks of its kind in the world — five times larger (thirty-one miles of shoreline) than New York's Central Park.

Above Right: A short-lived attraction, the Fiesta Bahia in Mission Bay drew thousands of participants and spectators for the festival on the water. This photo was taken at Bonita Cove in 1949.

Above Left: Highway 101, linking the seaside communities of Encinitas and Leucadia, has changed little since this photo was taken in 1950. Above Right: In its hey-dey, from the 1930s through the 1950s, Belmont Park at Mission Beach was a center for recreation, outdoor music and dancing. John D. Spreckels' plan for a plunge, ballroom and other first-class seashore amusements changed direction after his death, and gradually the park declined.

The San Diego Zoological Society shed the model of the typical city zoo and acquired worldwide fame. The society added to the preservation of wild life by opening the scientific and recreational Wild Animal Park at San Pasqual, near Escondido.

On April 15, 1947, voters went to the polls after Mayor Harley Knox had fought for the revival of the Nolen Plan for the Cedar Street Mall, a complex of ten to twenty public buildings including a new library, school administration center, hall of justice, and convention center. The plan went down to defeat.

Interest continued on growth questions for a city of beauty and one efficiently run through sound planning—planning well in advance of crises times. By 1949, however, voters were hesitant to go too far, and again in that year the Nolen Plan lost.

The harbor front took on a new look. The waterfront south from Market Street to National City turned largely to industry. The harbor north of the city-county administration building later included man-made Harbor and Shelter Islands with hotels, parks, marinas, recreation, and sports areas. In between the main piers, hotels and restaurants fronted the bay; a fleet of historic maritime vessels and berths for the commercial fishing fleet greeted visitors to the harbor.

The tuna industry continued to be fraught with dangers despite technological changes. Clippers could range fifteen thousand miles to search for schools of fish spotted by helicopter. Yet sophisticated radar and communications systems could not cope with the ferocity of *churabascos* (Pacific storms). In 1956 the crew of the

Anthony M. developed the power block and nylon nets which improved catching skills immensely to help the business thrive.

Imports of Japanese tuna in 1947 cut into the market; seizures of American ships in foreign waters at the slighest of excuses continued to be costly as competing nations levied fines. Environmentalists forced limits on the number of porpoise that could be taken in nets, and one species of tuna, the yellowfin, travels with certain species of porpoise thus limiting the yellowfin catch.

Heavy traffic from the growing suburbs began to strain city streets, but in a period of slight recession voters continued to turn down public improvements. Outmoded streetcars, ferryboats, and other forms of transportation, which had been adequate during the war years, now added to the congestion and a need for change.

The many servicemen stationed in San Diego during World War II routinely succumbed to the frivolous distractions of Belmont Park.

San Diego
Becomes a City

A popular resort for the rich and fashionable, Hotel Agua Caliente in Baja California attracted many visitors from the United States, thus increasing the flow of profitable tourist trade through the San Diego area. The gateway to the hotel is shown here in this 1934 photograph.

In 1948 a freeway cut through Balboa Park and reduced park lands. The need for the road had become critical to the growth of the city, and the question was how to move traffic from the suburbs to downtown without dissecting a neighborhood. Struggles throughout the region over valuable park and canyon lands became a key environmental issue after that time.

By April 23, 1949, the last of the electric streetcars made their runs, and within two years the San Diego and Arizona Railway chose to discontinue passenger service. Buses on city streets, filling the air with exhaust fumes and noise pollution, only served to dramatize the problem of heavy traffic from the suburbs.

Much of San Diego's charm is in its setting. Natural canyons such as Maple, Florida, and San Clemente have been left intact allowing open space to add to the freshness and cleanliness of the city.

Pioneer horticulturist Kate Sessions, a graduate of the University of California at Berkeley, planted a variety of vegetation in some of these areas, which have become havens for hawks and deer, skunks and opossums. Hikers, joggers, and picnickers mingle with the scientists who search for evidence of Pliocene whales, sharks, and sea life long ago embedded on the canyon slopes.

Mission Valley, the largest and lushest of the city's canyons, had an unlimited potential as a recreational area united with Mission Bay Park, but a most dramatic loss of environmental resources occurred with the opening of the first motel there in 1953 and when a major east-west freeway cut through the valley floor.

A company determined to build in the "Valley of the Padres" sought rezoning of agricultural-residential areas to accommodate commercial interests. A spokesman told the city council, "The Company promises to build in keeping with the beauty and history of the valley, and the buildings will breathe the spirit of the missions."

The council changed codes to allow development of the valley over strong voices which argued that the beautiful area would gradually become one huge shopping complex from the sea to the mountains. In time, hotels, motels, Westgate Plaza, and a voter-approved Westgate Park Stadium arose from the riverbed on concrete platforms. Sand and gravel pits had already eroded the river bottoms and eaten away the slopes to the north. A yard for old automobile bodies and junk covered sites in view of Mission San Diego de Alcalá where once sat *rancherias*.

In 1959 Joseph E. Jessop brought together sixty businessmen to form San Diegans Inc., to revitalize the downtown area. The plan was to build a center for the city's cultural, financial, and administrative activities. Urban renewal was considered too controversial at this time so financing was a major problem. Their quick success with this complex inspired other similarly organized civic and neighborhood committees.

Above: Delores Del Rio performed in a 1928 version of Helent Hunt Jackson's Ramona. This photograph depicts promotional efforts by KGB radio station in front of the downtown San Diego theater hosting the performance. Left: Crates of fruit being delivered for a Christmas party at Lindbergh Field. This photograph was taken on December 20, 1936.

San Diego
Becomes a City

A decade later a Sierra Club chapter worked at preserving parks and open space with Citizens Coordinate for Century Three (San Diego's third century began in 1969).

At the end of the decade most outlying areas had experienced building booms linking new shopping areas and centers to the freeways. The shopping center race had been stimulated by the first crosstown freeway in 1955 which cut off part of Balboa Park and took the heart out of Middletown's Victorian buildings and the Italian community. Those freeways would eventually lead to shopping centers at College Grove, Grossmont Center, South Bay, Clairemont, Parkway Plaza, University Town Centre, and other suburbs of the future.

Opposite: Fishing boats finally outnumbered troop transports in 1951. Above: In 1950 the first views a visitor faced moving up-town included the Broadway wharf, the eleventh Naval District Headquarters, Lane Field, home of the Padres Pacific Coast Baseball Team and the Santa Fe Depot.

San Diego
Becomes a City

On September 15, 1887, the San Diego Daily Bee reported that architects Clements and Stannard, with contractor J.H. Harding, would build a three-story, brick-veneered structure with galvanized iron cornices, iron columns and plate glass fronts with balconies surrounding the second and third stories for a sum of $18,000. The project resulted in the Grand Pacific Hotel at Fifth and J streets. Over the years the hotel has accommodated office and restaurant space and permanent as well as nightly residency. In its location at the south end of the historic Gaslamp Quarter, it has been remarkably restored to match the area's decor.

Chapter 10

Development of the City Beautiful

URING THE STORMY sixties, the nation became polarized over the Vietnam conflict; environmental questions, ethnic struggles, and student unrest occupied newspaper space. An additional concern in San Diego was cleaning up the city.

Businessmen were concerned about city planning for the future of the entire region as well as for special interest areas. That meant solving such problems as pockets of poverty, unemployment levels, rising crime rates, arson, and increasing the kinds of businesses that would blend well with the city. These leaders recognized the principal sources of income as the aircraft industry, tuna fishing and canning, shipbuilding, tourism, and the armed forces.

There had been a growing effort to diversify the kinds of employment, to prevent the city from being top-heavy in one area of economics, to preclude the disastrous situations which occurred in cities where heavy industry was a prime employer.

Could not the city's future be strengthened in commerce and finance, government activities in research and education, in the professions, and in retirement living? To give direction to such ideas and to project the future of the city, various civic organizations commissioned studies.

Planning for Balboa Park and Mission Bay Park continued as voters approved $12,600,000 in bonds for the Mission Bay ex-

In the field of education, San Diego, like the rest of the state, experienced an explosion of new institutions boasting world-renowned faculties. The University of California at San Diego, above, opened its campus in 1964 on 1,000 acres of verdant La Jolla countryside. The University of San Diego in Alcalá Park, opposite top, began as separate units in 1949 and 1952, merging into a major private university in 1972. Each institution is particularly notable and attracts qualified educators in such fields as oceanography, archaeology, physics and medicine.

San Diego
An Illustrated History

198

pansion. As early as 1961 the council moved to acquire downtown land to centralize public buildings at the same time the court house was being completed. Between 1928 and 1960 not a single office building had gone up in the center of the city.

The "Spreckels" downtown began to change in 1961 with a few high-rise office buildings replacing older structures. The construction helped to sustain a sagging local economy. The city council, led by Mayor Frank Curran, and the county board of supervisors, working with citizens advisory groups, studied the need for a community concourse, the improvement of Lindbergh Field as a major jet airport, and made efforts to woo light, smokeless industry to the area.

Planners recognized that the continued population growth required expansion of public buildings. In 1964 the sixteen-million-dollar Convention and Performing Arts Center, which included the City Administration Building and Civic Theatre, was completed downtown by the city without a public bond issue or a vote, using a combination of employee retirement funds and private donations from downtown businesses. In 1965 the centralized Charles C. Dail Community Concourse was dedicated, and the theater, designed by Ruocco, Kennedy and Rosser, opened.

One serious deficiency in the intellectual climate, however, had been the earlier placement of the main public library away from the center of government activities. It does not serve as a major respository for local government records, nor a managed archives, which many major cities have long regarded as crucial for the preservation of research materials vital to the direction of the city.

The formation of the state legislature of the Unified Port District in 1962 with San Diego Harbor Commission, reaffirmed the intent to watch over and develop the use of one of the world's most spectacular harbors. Marine terminal developments and industrial areas would have to skirt certain areas of the harbor.

Sea World, created in 1964, and a Mission Bay Reclamation Project with marinas, hotels, and docks within the forty-six-hundred-acre Mission Bay Park came under construction at a cost of thirty-two million dollars. Sea World, an aquatic park built at a cost of six million dollars, showed one way in which the climate, clean air, and ocean life offered unparalleled opportunities in recreation-oriented occupations.

In 1965 San Diego became the sixteenth largest city in the United States in population. Freeways gave access from various points in the city to the Escondido Village Shopping Mall and development communities at Rancho Bernardo and Los Penasquitos. Electronic firms moved to industrial parks. The Veterans Administration built its hospital near the University of California at San Diego School of Medicine. In 1924, Scripps Clinic opened as a small medical facility; some fifty years later it became dedicated as the Scripps Clinic and Research Foundation.

Above: The United States International University at Camp Elliott is a few miles northeast of San Diego nestled in the eucalyptus groves of what had once been the Scripps estate.

The Development of
the City Beautiful

Point Loma College is the outgrowth of educational work begun in Los Angeles in 1902 by Dr. Phineas F. Bresee, a founder of the Church of the Nazarene. The institution was incorporated as Pacific Bible College in northeast Pasadena and came to be known as Pasadena College. In 1973 the college relocated on Point Loma and its name therefore changed to Point Loma College.

The Salk Institute for Biological Research founded in 1963, complemented both the University of California at San Diego and the Scripps Institution of Oceanography, a marine biological institution at the head of Rose Canyon near La Jolla.

Mayor Curran saw these developments as reaffirming San Diego's determination to avoid "dependence on industry." The City of San Diego Community Concourse was the beginning of the grouping of public buildings, and the bus system became public in 1966 with help from the federal government. As he looked to the future of the city, Mr. Curran said, "We'll not surrender to the auto."

In the mid-sixties the merging of major corporations came about. On March 30, 1953, Convair control passed to General Dynamics Corporation, and by 1956 it had entered space-age industry with huge contracts, opening a plant on Kearny Mesa. But in 1965, thousands of employees were laid off; San Diego experienced a bust in levels of employment. Since then General Dynamics has become one of the major space-age corporations in San Diego.

Solar Aircraft became part of Harvester International, and General Atomic became the property of a major oil company, reflecting a change in style of operations. Ryan Aeronautical Company today operates as a subsidiary of Teledyne Inc., under the name Teledyne Ryan Aeronautical in the fields of aerospace and electric technology.

The financial institution which had existed the longest as a home town business was the San Diego Trust and Savings Bank. A few others had been in San Diego for some time: The Bank of America, First National Bank, and the U.S. National Bank. Now came the banks from the North. At first institutions themselves opened branches, but by 1970 the merging of banks began, and

new banks emerged like the Women's Bank and the Mexican-American Bank which were aimed at minorities. These were joined by the Bank of Tokyo of California, California Canadian Bank, Japan California, Lloyds Bank California, and Sumitomo Bank of California. The promotion of San Diego as a financial center, so essential to community growth, had at last begun to evolve.

Funds for the construction of Hoover Dam on the Colorado River had been approved during President Coolidge's administration. Years later when water was needed it was close by, carried through an aqueduct to Los Angeles. The first barrel of a double pipe-line to San Diego was finished in 1947 and was soon taxed to capacity. In 1952–1954 the second barrel was completed, but the need for water grew.

While the world has marveled over the Roman, Babylonian, and Carthagenian aqueducts, water systems in this country have carried water over greater obstacles and longer distances.

The arid southwest with its population explosion commanded the use of more and more water. Voters in 1966 gave approval to the San Diego County Water Authority to approve financing for distribution of Feather River water, five hundred miles north in San Diego County, and approved thirty million dollars to construct the second pipeline of the second San Diego aqueduct, completed to the Miramar Reservoir.

San Diego State University was founded March 13, 1897, to train elementary school teachers. Following reorganization as a four-year state teacher's college, and cooperation by the legislature and city to provide a new site, the burgeoning campus moved to seven Mission style buildings surrounding the Main Quad (above right) on the outskirts of the city in 1931. The open-faced bell tower and archway of Hepner Hall distinguish the photo at left. In 1971 the name was changed from San Diego State College to San Diego State University.

The Development of the City Beautiful

Construction of the Civic Center and Community Concourse marked a new era for downtown San Diego in the mid 1960s. Prior to then, not a single office building had been constructed in center city since 1928. Giving thought to San Diego's position as sixteenth largest U.S. city in population in 1965, city planners ruled that centralization of public buildings would relieve dependence on the automobile.

Voters approved a new twenty-seven-million-dollar sports stadium in Mission Valley in 1966. In that same year the International Sports Arena was built near Mission Bay Park, and in January of that year, when San Diegans Inc. met, they saw one solution to the declining downtown as urban renewal. That body virtually served as a redevelopment agency for a year.

San Diegans approved the modified general plan in 1967. Frank E. Curran, reelected as mayor in November 1967, deftly indicated it would ony be a guide for the growth of San Diego. The San Onofre Nuclear Generating Station became an on-going bone of contention between environmentalists and scientists involved with energy; neither group has ever presented a strong case for its side.

In celebration of the two-hundredth birthday of San Diego, concessionaires hastily erected one of Columbus's vessels in the Old Town plaza as the symbol of the founding of California, rather than a replica of the ill-fated *San José*. The city neglected to allow scientists to excavate and restore the Spanish Royal Pre-

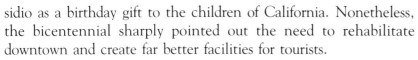

sidio as a birthday gift to the children of California. Nonetheless, the bicentennial sharply pointed out the need to rehabilitate downtown and create far better facilities for tourists.

The Old Town State Historic Park, a dream of State Senator and historian James Mills, became a reality in his time. By 1969, most of the property had been acquired and restoration of buildings began once the temporary celebration structures had been torn down.

In 1969 the orthotropic* Coronado Bay Bridge opened; at the same time the ferryboats introduced before the turn of the century made their final crossing to the disappointment of the many people who had enjoyed the leisurely ten-minute ride across the bay.

In that year the U.S. Department of the Interior awarded San Diego the Clear Water Award for the bay, which was considered to be the cleanest urban estuary in the nation. This had come about because the San Diego sewage treatment plant, completed in Point Loma in 1962, had begun to recover more than fifty years' accumulation of bay pollution.

At the turn of the decade, in 1970, San Diego's population had risen to fourteenth largest in the country as the "M" Factor (migration) increased. Neil Morgan's "Westward Tilt" accelerated with each passing year.

In a second rezoning, Fashion Valley opened in 1969; the creation of another shopping center brought the total to nine in the county.

In 1971 construction continued to improve the appearance of the city. Security Pacific Plaza and the Bank of California each erected an eighteen-story downtown high-rise office building. Assemblyman Pete Wilson was elected mayor of San Diego. The

*having the longer axis more or less vertical.

Above Left: The Lindbergh Air Terminal, located southwest of the field, opened in 1967 followed by a second terminal in 1979. For twenty years community residents have reopened the question of whether to move the field to an outlying area. Proximity to business, recreational and residential areas provokes an argument on both sides of the issue. Above Right: The Star of India *celebrated America's Bicentennial in full sail. As the oldest merchantman afloat, she has rounded the world twenty-seven times since her launching at Ramsey in the Isle of Man. For some years interested San Diegans spotted her berthed at the waterfront and raised the funds to drydock, restore and elevate her to the central figure in the Maritime Museum at the foot of B Street.*

The Development of the City Beautiful

Royal Inn at the Wharf and the new U.S. Post Office on Midway Drive, along with other significant structures, were another part of the facelift the city badly needed.

Despite an emphasis on hotel room additions for tourists and conventions in 1972, the city lost the Republican National Convention because of the lack of hotel accommodations. Yet 1972 was the county's first billion-dollar building year.

Redevelopment projects authorized by the city council in 1972 encompassed eighty-one city blocks. By the next year decisions had to be made to halt a very rapid growth that threatened to spur serious urban problems. Given the best of conditions, the city and county could not have handled the public services and utilities crises created by urban growth that had taken place too rapidly.

By April 1975, when Pete Wilson was reelected mayor, voters gave tacit approval to a policy to manage the city's planned growth considered to be among the most stringent in the United States. It meant to not only control the urban sprawl but the decay of the inner city as well. An ordinance was passed which required all home construction to be coordinated with availability of municipal services. At this time the city council (which is the Redevelopment Agency) created Centre City Development Corporation to direct the redevelopment of downtown San Diego.

At almost the same time Hamilton Marston (descendant of the indomitable George White Marston) and the Marston family commissioned Kevin Lynch and Donald Appleyard to take "a look at the special landscape of the San Diego region." The two urban specialists turned out a remarkable report they titled *Temporary Paradise?*, in which the possessed assets of San Diego were pointed out and a way to manage them was suggested.

Advertising campaigns which referred to San Diego as "America's Finest City," brought year-round tourists, and businesses earned five billion dollars per year from the tourist industry. By 1977 the city ranked ninth in the nation in population.

The year 1978 turned out to be tragic for San Diegans. Arsonists destroyed both the Aerospace Museum and the Old Globe Theatre in Balboa Park in the month of February. The theater, created for the 1935 exposition, was a reproduction of Shakespeare's original.

One of the worst disasters in American airline history took place in September when Pacific Southwest Airlines Flight 182 from Sacramento to San Diego collided with a private plane over North Park. The accident claimed the lives of 144 persons and sparked anew the controversey over the location of Lindbergh Field so close to town.

At the onset of the 1980s San Diego ranked eighth in population. To follow the planned growth policy required agreement during the 1970s among the developers, the environmentalists, and governmental agencies.

The alter ego of the Redevelopment Agency, the Centre City Development Corporation, has a number of projects to carry out—largely what four generations of planners have been working to-

Space-age technology firms are discovering an enthusiastic climate for operation in San Diego. In 1980 the value of aerospace products manufactured in San Diego totaled $919,630,000. That figure doesn't include the aerospace output from electronics companies.

The Development of
the City Beautiful

Built just before the Grand Pacific Hotel (left) the Long-Waterman House was designed by architects Benson and Reif. Located at 2408 First Avenue, the three-story Queen Anne Victorian home was built for Kate and John S. Long who owned a lumber business in Coronado. In 1893 Robert Waterman, governor of California from 1887 to 1891, bought the home for $17,000. Presently it is owned by Parker Industries and has been completely restored as office facilities for the company. The domed Queen Anne towers, lace-like handrailing and adjacent carriage house are showcase features.

ward and which will take that same style of cooperation among those concerned.

The Horton Plaza Redevelopment, a major in-town project with shopping, hotels, offices, and residences, has been slow to move because of delays in land acquisition, financing problems, and questions raised by preservationists.

The Marina/Columbia Redevelopment Project is designed to provide residential living and to serve as a link from the business center to the foot of Broadway. The Columbia area includes the historic Santa Fe Depot and emphasizes a convention center, hotels, and offices. These regions are close to Seaport Village, a fourteen-million-dollar shopping, dining, and recreational complex, built on twenty-two acres of waterfront land at the foot of Pacific Highway and Harbor Drive, completed in 1979–1980.

The future of the Convention Center project was again tested in 1981 by a mail vote on the $225-million project, the most expensive in city history, but visibly the most dynamic and needed of the projects. A negative vote reflected the conservative attitude of San Diegans who appeared puzzled by the method of financing.

The matter is not dead. The enormity of the changes for San Diego must be made clearer next time around.

A major successful project, the rehabilitation of a sixteen-block, thirty-eight-acre Gaslamp Quarter National Historic District is in progress. As of April 1980, more than thirty-two million dollars in private funds had gone into restoring the architectural beauties of the past. Turn-of-the-century street lighting, street fur-

niture, landscaping, and other improvements in progress are turn-ing a once-blighted area into one of the city's jewels. A dynamic citizen's project area committee appointed by the city council is spearheading the project.

In 1975 the city council approved plans for a San Diego streetcar line made up of sixteen miles of track to run from the Santa Fe Depot to the San Ysidro border. A portion of the system is to run through the city and tie in at the main system on Harbor Drive. The trolley line which opened to the public in July, 1981 incudes a proposed Gaslamp-area trolley to make a circuit in town and through the Gaslamp Quarter.

San Diego is still the home of the largest military complex in the United States. It is a city where aerospace industry is the lead-ing source of civilian employment and where electronic firms are the manufacturing leaders; health sciences and other forms of high technology, research-oriented industries are not far behind.

Pressures of urbanization are pushing land and housing prices upward. The attraction of unusual profits through converting lands for housing is reducing the vacant space. Yet agricultural acreage and gross receipts from farming are on the rise. It would appear that despite consumption of open space, agriculture will have ample room to grow at this pace into the twenty-first century.

There is a cultural and economic interchange between San Diego and Tia Juana; there is communication among organizations, citizens, and politicians. Some thirty-five to forty million visitors cross the border annually — a tremendous volume of traffic across

Above Left: The Yuma Building is one of the earliest brick struc-tures in the Gaslamp Quarter. Built approximately 1882 for owner Alfred Henry Wilcox, the building didn't achieve its full three-story height until 1888. It has been pristinely restored by architects Macy, Henderson and Cole who operate from the property. Above: Seaport Village Ltd. leased its acreage from the San Diego Unified Port District in 1978. The corporation, headed by developer Bryant Morris, contractor Sheldon Pol-lac and financier Morris Taub-man, developed the fourteen-million-dollar-center after a sea-faring motif.

The Development of
the City Beautiful

Top: Looking down Fourth
Street at the area once known
as "Banker's Hill," the view

stretches to the Coronado Bay
Bridge and the peninsula beyond.
Above:
Reflected lights dance across the
bay in this nighttime panorama
which reaches to Point Loma. The
surrounding canyons and Balboa

Park's central position enhance
urban living.

any international boundary line anywhere. One could envision by the turn of the new century, a large bicultural international city, a merger of Tia Juana and San Diego, the two cities having grown close enough together to share the same facilities and tourists.

The quality of life in Baja California should improve during the 1980s as long neglected sewage, trash, road, and water problems are being dealt with in massive urban development. The rehabilitation of *Avenida Revolución* is part of the improvement by Tia Juana's public works. Federal grants and loans, in addition to state and city funding, are being made available in getting the work done. Tia Juana's 9.5 percent annual growth rate has contributed to a breakdown in services that could not keep up with the new populations, forcing city planners to redesign public facilities.

During the 1980s the Mexican government's projects include relocation of squatters to make way for a national park, construction of a shopping center, building an aqueduct to carry drinking water from the Colorado River and Mexicali Valley, and the paving of a river flood-control channel.

One area of growth, however, still needs the attention of community leaders. To any degree major companies do not yet

Above Left: The Imperial Bank Tower is San Diego's largest office building to date, measuring 600,000 square feet and rising to twenty-four stories. Recessed windows mark the sixth and twenty-second levels of the globular structure at Seventh and B streets. Above and Above Right: The twenty-seven-story Columbia Centre is scheduled for completion in 1982. The commercial structure will house a seven-story atrium.

Property for Old Town State Historical Park was acquired in 1969, followed by restoration of San Diego's finest historic buildings. A section of Old San Diego Avenue, closed to automobiles, is a haven for pedestrians and horse-drawn surreys. Visitors can tour the restored structures and sample quaint shops and restaurants.

have headquarters in San Diego. A few do, but for the most part, major decisions relating to San Diego by corporations are made elsewhere. This is unfortunate because San Diego is a city that one must see and live in to appreciate its potential.

Certainly the defense posture of the Reagan administration in 1981 must be clear to those wondering about the future of government spending. Currently more than eight hundred businesses in the county have defense contracts.

Research and development firms — the problem solvers — have found a home in the county, along with a variety of construction, space-age equipment, shipbuilding, and engine manufacturing companies which will continue to create hundreds of jobs and promote the kind of industry palatable to the local residents.

As the twenty-first century nears, it becomes clear that there are many immigrants knocking at the gates to Horton's "Heaven-on-Earth." As the population increases so do the demands for public services and for housing. To meet these rapidly expanding needs, there must be cooperative interplay among political influences, the construction industry, and financial powers, in order to manage solutions within the San Diego landscape.

Top: Mission Bay Park is popular with fishermen who like to catch their dinner along the bay's twenty-seven miles of beaches. Above: Seaport Village includes shops, business offices, and restaurants. Left: The San Diego Zoo acquired far-reaching fame when it pioneered natural settings for animals, familiar now in zoos around the world.

The Development of the City Beautiful

Top Left: This masterpiece in sand rose from a San Diego beach as part of a sand-castle building contest. Contestants included amateurs as well as professional artists, architects and planners.

Above Left: Devotees of sailing are addicted to San Diego's bays, harbors and marinas. Boats of every shape and size ply the waters, offering not only sport but home to those who choose to live aboard.

Above Right: Gaslamps mark the seventeen-block district undergoing

restoration to preserve turn-of-the-century buildings. The effort is a joint venture of the government and private enterprise.

San Diego
An Illustrated History

The local government has a history of being well run, of functioning as a clean government. Additionally, San Diego is a city unmatched anywhere else for its citizen involvement.

When the conquistadors looked to this land for fulfillment of their adventurous dreams they found no gold and silver, no Amazon queen, no earthly city of wealth.

What they did find was indeed a terrestrial paradise and their stories show they recognized it as such. What they could not have known is that they were the vanguard of immigrants from every part of the world, who brought the best of their cultural heritage and that their descendants would discover true wealth in this city — riches in climate, environment, natural resources, and opportunity.

The fabulous Hotel del Coronado was the brainchild of Indiana-born Elisha Babcock. He looked over the desolate Coronado peninsula in 1885 and decided it was the ideal spot for his million-dollar hotel and residential community. Three years later the multi-turreted structure lured not only visitors to Coronado, but home-buyers who purchased more than a million dollars' worth of lots.

The Development of
the City Beautiful

Illustration and Photo Credits

Bibliography

Adams, H. Austin. *The Man John D. Spreckels*. San Diego: Frye & Smith, 1924.

Adams, John R. *San Diego Authors*. San Diego: San Diego State College Press, 1960.

Anonymous. *The City and County of San Diego*. San Diego: Leberthon and Taylor, 1888.

Anonymous. *An Illustrated History of Southern California*. Chicago: The Lewis Publishing Company, 1890.

Archives of California, in 63 volumes on 63 reels of microfilm at the Bancroft Library, University of California, Berkeley.

Bancroft, Hubert Howe. *History of California, 1542 – 1890*. 7 volumes. San Francisco: The History Company, 1884–1890.

Bartlett, John Russell. *Personal Narrative of Explorations and Incidents in Texas, New Mexico, California, Sonora and Chihuahua Connected with the United States and Mexico Boundary Commission during the years, 1859, 51, 52 and 53*. 2 volumes. Chicago: Rio Grande Press Inc., 1965.

Baur, John E. *The Health Seekers of Southern California, 1870 – 1890*. San Marino, California: The Huntington Library, 1959.

Beechey, Captain F. M. *An Account of a Visit to California, 1826 – 1827*. San Francisco: Grabhorn Press, 1941.

Bigger, Richard and others. *Metropolitan Coast: San Diego and Orange Counties, California*. Los Angeles, Bureau of Governmental Research, University of California, 1958.

Black, Samuel F. *History of San Diego, California: A Record of Settlement, Organization Progress, and Achievement*. 3 volumes. Chicago: S. J. Clarke Publishing Company, 1913.

Booth, Larry. *Portrait of a Boom Town, San Diego in the 1880's* (by Larry Booth, Roger Olmstead and Richard F. Pourade). San Diego: San Diego Historical Society, 1971.

Brandes, Ray. "Mission San Diego de Alcalá: Archaeological and Historical Discoveries," in *Some Catholic Reminiscences for the United States Bicentennial*. Edited by Msgr. Francis J. Weber, Catholic Conference of California by the Knights of Columbus, 1976.

Britt, Albert. *Ellen Browning Scripps: Journalist and Idealist*. Great Britain: Oxford University Press, 1960.

Carter, George F. *Pleistocene Man at San Diego*. Baltimore: The Johns Hopkins Press, 1957.

Clark, Dwight. *Stephen Watts Kearny: Soldier of the West*. Norman: University of Oklahoma Press, 1961.

Cole, Martin and Welcome, Henry, eds. *Don Pio Pico's Historical Narrative*. Translated by Arthur E. Botello. Glendale: Arthur H. Clark Company, 1973.

Costansó, Miguel. *The Costansó Narrative of the Portola Expedition: First Chronicle of the Spanish Conquest of Alta California*. Edited and translated by Ray Brandes. Newhall, California: Hogarth Press, 1972.

Cotton, Oscar W. *The Good Old Days*. New York: The Exposition Press Inc., 1962.

Dana, Richard Henry. *Two Years Before the Mast: A Personal Narrative of Life at Sea (1834–1836)*. Edited by John Haskell Kemble. Los Angeles: Ward Ritchie Press, 1964.

Davis, William Heath. *Seventy Five Years in California*. San Francisco: John Howell, 1967.

Derby, George. *Phoenixiana*. San Francisco: Grabhorn Press, 1937.

Dodge, Richard V. *Rails of the Silver Gate: The Spreckels San Diego Empire*. San Diego: Pacific Railway Journal, 1960.

Drake, Sir Francis. *The World Encompassed*. Readex Microprint Corporation. c1966. Reprint of 1628 work.

Dumke, Glenn S. *The Boom of the Eighties in Southern California*. San Marino: The Huntington Library, 1944.

Elliott, W. W. *History of San Diego County*. San Francisco: Elliott Publishers, 1883.

Emory, William H. *Notes of a Military Reconnaissance from Fort Leavenworth in Missouri to San Diego in California including parts of Arkansas, Del Norte and Gila River*. Washington, 1848: Wendell and Van Benthuysen.

Engelhardt, Zephyrin, O.F.M. *San Diego Mission*. San Francisco: James H. Barry Co., 1920.

Engstrand, Iris W. and Brandes, Ray. *Old Town San Diego, 1821–1874*. San Diego: Alcalá Press, 1976.

Engstrand, Iris H. W. *San Diego, California's Cornerstone*. Tulsa: Continental Heritage Press Inc., 1980.

Eyer, Marguerite, ed. *Duflot de Mofras' Travels on the Pacific Coast*. Santa Ana: Fine Arts Press, 1927.

Fages, Pedro. *A Historical, Political, and Natural Description of California by Pedro Fages, Soldier of Spain*. Translated by Herbert Ingram Priestly. Berkeley: University of California Press, 1937.

Federal Writers' Project. *San Diego, California*. San Diego: San Diego Historical Society, 1937.

Fletcher, Col. Ed. *Memoirs of Ed Fletcher*. San Diego: Pioneer Printers, c1952.

Flint, Timothy, ed. *The Personal Narrative of James O. Pattie of Kentucky*. Chicago: The Lakeside Press, 1930.

Gardner, Gilson. *Lusty Scripps: The Life of E. W. Scripps*. New York: The Vanguard Press, 1932.

Gast, Ross H. *Don Francisco de Paula Marin: A Biography*. The Letters and Journal of Francisco de Paula Marin edited by Agnes C. Conrad. Honolulu: The University Press of Hawaii, 1973.

Geiger, Maynard J. *The Life and Times of Fray Junipero Serra*. Washington, D.C.: Academy of American Franciscan History, 1959.

Gerhard, Peter. *Pirates on the West Coast of New Spain, 1575–1742*. Glendale: Arthur H. Clark Company, 1960.

Goodhue, Bertram G. *The Architecture and the Gardens of the San Diego Exposition*. San Francisco: Paul Elder and Co., 1916.

Greenwalt, Emmett A. *The Point Loma Community in California.* Berkeley: University of California Press, 1955.

Griffin, Dr. John S. *A Doctor Comes to California: The diary of John S. Griffin, 1846–1847.* San Francisco: California Historical Society, 1953.

Gudde, Erwin G. *Bigler's Chronicle of the West.* Berkeley: University of California Press, 1962.

Heilbron, Carl H., ed. *History of San Diego County.* San Diego: San Diego Press Club, 1936.

Heizer, Robert and Whipple, M. A., eds. *The California Indians: A Source Book.* Berkeley: University of California Press, 1965.

Henderson, John D., ed. *San Diego American Institute of America Guide Book.* San Diego: AIA, c1972.

Higgins, Shelley J. *This Fantastic City.* San Diego: City of San Diego, 1956.

Homes, Maurice G. *From New Spain by Sea to the Californias, 1519–1668.* Glendale: Arthur H. Clark Company, 1963.

Hopkins, Harry C. *History of San Diego: Its Pueblo Lands and Water.* San Diego: City Printing Company, 1929.

James, George Wharton. *Exposition Memories, Panama-California Exposition, San Diego, 1916.* Pasadena: The Radiant Life Press, 1967.

————. *Exposition Memories.* Pasadena: Radiant Life Press, 1917.

Kettner, William. *Why It Was Done and How.* Compiled by Mary B. Steyle. San Diego: Frye & Smith, 1923.

Kirsch, Robert and Murphy, William S. *West of the West.* New York: E. P. Dutton and Co., Inc., 1947.

Kroeber, Alfred L. *Handbook of the Indians of California.* Smithsonian Institution, Bureau of American Ethnology Bulletin 78. Washington, D.C.: Government Printing Office, 1925.

Los Angeles Star, 1860–1861.

MacMullen, Jerry. *They Came By Sea: A Pictorial History of San Diego Bay.* San Diego: Ward Ritchie Press and the Maritime Association of San Diego, 1969.

Marston, Mary Gilman. *George White Marston: A Family Chronicle.* Los Angeles: Ward Ritchie Press, 2 volumes, 1956.

Mathes, W. Michael, ed. *The Capture of the Santa Ana at Cabo San Lucas, November 1587.* Los Angeles: Dawson's Book Shop, 1969.

Mathes, W. Michael. *The Pearl Hunters in the Gulf of California, 1668.* Los Angeles: Dawson's Book Shop, 1966.

McCoy, Esther. *Five California Architects.* New York: Reinhold Publishing Company, New York, 1960.

McGrew, Clarence Alan. *Picturesque Old Town, City of San Diego, and San Diego County.* 2 volumes. Chicago: American Historical Society, 1922.

MacPhail, Elizabeth C. *The Story of New San Diego and of its Founder Alonzo E. Horton.* 2nd edition revised. National City: San Diego Historical Society, 1979.

Meigs, Peveril. *The Dominican Mission Frontier of Lower California.* Berkeley: University of California, 1935.

Miller, Henry. *Account of a Tour of the California Missions, 1856: The Journal and Drawings of Henry Miller.* The Book Club of California, 1952.

Mills, James. *San Diego — Where California Began.* San Diego: San Diego Historical Society, 1960.

———— *Historical Landmarks of San Diego County.* San Diego: San Diego Historical Society, 1959.

Minshall, Herbert L. *The Broken Stones.* Edited by Richard F. Pourade. San Diego: Union-Tribune Publishing Company c1976.

Minutes of the Common Council, City of San Diego, 1850–1900, Office of City Clerk, San Diego, California.

Morgan, Neil. *Westward Tilt: The American West Today.* New York: Random House, 1961.

Moriarty, James R. "Storms, Buccaneers and Sailing Ships on the California Coast, 1539–1779." *The Westerners,* San Diego Corral, July 1968.

———— . "The Coast Diegueno: San Diego's Historic Indian." *The Western Explorer,* December 1961.

Moyer, Cecil. *Historic Ranchos of San Diego.* Edited by Richard F. Pourade. San Diego, Union-Tribune Publishing Company, 1969.

Neuhaus, Eugene. *San Diego Garden Fair: The Art of the Exposition.* San Francisco: P. Elder and Co., 1916.

———— *San Diego Garden Fair; Personal Impressions of the Architecture, Sculpture, Horticulture, Color Scheme and other Aesthetic Aspects of the Panama California International Exposition.* San Francisco: P. Elder and Co., 1916.

Nolen, John. *San Diego, a Comprehensive Plan for its Improvement.* A condensation by Samuel Wood Hamill of the Cambridge, Mass., edition of 1908. San Diego: San Diegans Inc., 1960.

Orbach, Michael K. *Hunters, Seamen, and Entrepreneurs: The Tuna Seinermen of San Diego.* Berkeley: University of California Press, 1977.

Palou, Fr. Francisco, O.F.M. *Historical Memoirs of New California.* Edited by Herbert Eugene Bolton. Berkeley: University of California Press, 1926.

Phillips, George Harwood. *Chiefs and Challengers: Indian Resistance and Cooperation in Southern California.* San Marino: Huntington Library, 1975.

Pourade, Richard F. *The History of San Diego:*
Volume I. The Explorers, 1960.
Volume II. Time of the Bells, 1961.
Volume III. The Silver Dons, 1963.
Volume IV. The Glory Years, 1964.
Volume V. Gold in the Sun, 1965.
Volume VI. The Rising Tide, 1967.
Volume VII. City of the Dream, 1977.
Commissioned by James S. Copley, publisher. San Diego: Union-Tribune Publishing Company.

Powell, H. M. T. *The Santa Fe Trail to California, 1849–1852: The Journal and Drawings of H. M. T. Powell.* Edited by Douglas Sloane Watson. San Francisco Club of California, 1931.

Priestley, Herbert Ingram. *Franciscan Explorations in California.* Edited by Lillian Estelle Fisher. Glendale: Arthur H. Clark Company, 1946.

Records of the Alcalde and Ayuntamiento, 1826–1850. An index by Judge Benjamin Hayes, U.S. National Archives, Washington, D.C.

Requa, Richard S. *Inside Lights on the Building of San Diego's Exposition, 1935.* San Diego, c1937.

Robinson, Alfred. *Life in California During a Residence of Several Years in That Territory.* New York: DaCapo Press, 1969.

Rogers, Malcolm J. *Ancient Hunters of the Far West.* Edited by Richard F. Pourade. San Diego: Union-Tribune Publishing Company, 1966.

Rogers, Woodes. *A Cruising Voyage Around the World.* London: A. Bell, 1712.

Rolle, Andrew F. *An American in California: The Biography of William Heath Davis.* San Marino: Huntington Library, 1956.

———. *William Heath Davis and the Founding of American San Diego.* San Diego: Union Title and Trust Company, 1952.

Safley, J. C., ed. *The Copley Press.* San Diego: The Copley Press, Inc., 1953.

San Diego Magazine.

San Diego Daily Transcript.

San Diego Herald, 1851–1857.

San Diego Historical Society Quarterly, 1955–present (under several titles).

San Diego Evening-Tribune, 1895–present.

San Diego Sun, 1884–1939.

San Diego Union (daily and weekly), 1868–1874; 1871–present.

San Francisco California Star, 1848–1849.

Scott, Ed. *San Diego County Soldier-Pioneers, 1846–1866.* San Diego: County of San Diego, Bicentennial Project, 1976.

Schurz, William Lytle. *The Manila Galleon.* New York: E. P. Dutton and Co., Inc., 1959.

Smith, Cornelius, C., Jr., *Emilio Kosterlitzky: Eagle of Sonora and the Southwest Border.* Glendale: The Arthur H. Clark Company, 1979.

Smythe, William E. *History of San Diego.* San Diego: The History Company, 1906. In either 1 or 2 volumes.

Stewart, Don M. *Frontier Port.* Los Angeles: Ward Ritchie Press, 1966.

Sudsbury, Elretta. *Jackrabbits to Jets, The History of North Island,* San Diego, California. San Diego: Neyenesch Printers, c1967.

Sullivan, Susan. "James McCoy: Lawman and Legislator." *The Journal of San Diego History,* Vol. XXIII, No. 4, Fall 1977, pages 43–57.

Swanson, Walter S. *The Thin Gold Watch: A Personal History of the Newspaper Copleys.* New York: The Macmillan Company, 1964.

Taylor, Bayard. *El Dorado or Adventures in the Path of Empire.* New York: Alfred A. Knopf, 1949.

The Golden Era Magazine, 1887–1893.

Tibesar, Antonine, O.F.M. *The Writings of Junipera Serra.* 2 volumes. Washington, D.C.: Academy of American Franciscan History, 1955.

Tout, Otis B. *The First Thirty Years in Imperial Valley, California, 1901–1931.* San Diego: Arts and Crafts Press, 1931.

Tyler, Daniel. *A Concise History of the Mormon Battalion in the Mexican War, 1846–1847.* Chicago: The Rio Grande Press, 1964.

United States Department of the Interior. *Report on the U.S. and Mexican Boundary Survey made under the direction of the Secretary of the Interior by William H. Emory.* Washington, D.C.: A. O. P. Nicholson, printer, 1857–1859, 2 volumes.

United States War Department. *Reports of Explorations and Surveys to Ascertain the Most Practicable and Economical Route for a Railroad from the Mississippi River to the Pacific Ocean.* Made under the direction of the Secretary of War in 1853–1854, according to Acts of Congress, March 3, 1853, May 31, 1854, and August 5, 1854. Washington, D.C.: A. O. P. Nicholson, printer, 1855. Volumes 5 and 7.

Van Dyke, Theodore Strong. *The City and County of San Diego.* San Diego: Leberthon and Taylor, 1888.

———. *County of San Diego, the Italy of Southern California.* San Diego: San Diego Union Company, 1886.

Walker, Franklin D. *A Literary History of Southern California.* Berkeley: University of California Press, 1950.

Weber, Francis J. *Some California Catholic Reminiscences for The United States Bicentennial.* Los Angeles: Archdiocese of Los Angeles, 1976.

Watson, Douglas Sloane. *California in the Fifties: Views of Cities and Mining Towns in California and the West . . . .* San Francisco: J. Howell, 1936.

Whipple, Amiel Weeks. *Report of Explorations for a Railway Route Near the Thirty-Fifth Parallel of latitude from the Mississippi River to the Pacific Ocean.* Washington, D.C.: Government Printing Office, 1854.

Winslow, Carleton Monroe. *The Architecture and the Gardens of the San Diego Exposition: A Pictorial Survey of the Aesthetic Features of the Panama-California International Exposition. . . .* San Francisco: P. Elder and Company, 1916.

Wolcott, Marjorie Tisdale, ed. *Diaries of Judge Benjamin Hayes Pioneer Notes, 1849–1874.* Los Angeles: Privately Printed, 1929.

Woodward, Arthur, ed. *Journal of Lt. Thomas W. Sweeney, 1849–1853.* Los Angeles: Westernlore Press, 1956.

Index

Index

223